THE POWER BEHIND THE MIND

THE POWER BEHIND
THE MIND

Thirteen lectures on the
Yoga of Self-Knowledge

By

M. V. WATERHOUSE

SHANTI SADAN

LONDON

First published 1986 by Shanti Sadan

© Shanti Sadan
29 Chepstow Villas,
London W11 3DR

ISBN 0 85424 039 X

Printed and bound by Whitstable Litho Ltd.,
Whitstable, Kent.

'Become what you are!'

Orphic saying

CONTENTS

FOREWORD

THOSE who have read *Training the Mind through Yoga*, the collection of fourteen lectures by Miss M V Waterhouse first published in 1964, will need no introduction to the present book which contains thirteen of her hitherto unpublished talks on Adhyatma Yoga, the Yoga of Self-Knowledge. Marjorie Waterhouse was one of the earliest and closest pupils of Hari Prasad Shastri, an acknowledged master of Yoga, having joined him soon after he arrived in England from the East in July 1929. After his death in 1956, she became the second Warden of Shanti Sadan, the Centre of Adhyatma Yoga in London, and she held this post for the following seven years.

She brought to her understanding of the philosophy and practice of the spiritual Yoga a practical attitude which was more concerned with smoothing the difficulties of the ordinary man in his attempts to control and enlighten his mind than with the abstruse metaphysical questions posed by the Vedanta philosophy. One of her striking sayings was: 'We do not yet love the human heart sufficiently.' But she herself was one of the people least open to this charge. Her sympathy and common sense were enlivened by a delightful sense of humour, which finds expression even on the printed page.

Practical Yoga, as she says, is the process of transforming the mind through meditation, purification and self-control, and involves facing up to, and dealing effectively with, many obstacles which the raw and untutored mind puts up in the way of resistance to change. The transition from individuality to universality is not achieved without effort and without giving up many of the wrong ways of thought which bedevil our ordinary thinking. In this process, the greatest need of the would-be yogi is for sound guidance and clear advice, and this he will get in abundance from the pages of this book.

I

CONSCIOUS LIVING

YOGA is not a religion, nor a system of philosophy, but it is the method by which the goal of a religion or a philosophy may be realised and the spiritual purpose of man may be achieved. That purpose is direct cognition of his true nature, which is divine. Yoga is, of necessity, practical, for it is not an end in itself, but the means to an end, and when that end has been reached then the task of Yoga has been fulfilled and it can be laid aside, as all training and discipline is laid aside once a learner has become an adept.

There are many authentic, that is, traditional Yogas. Adhyatma Yoga is based on the Advaita or non-dual system of thought, which postulates an all-pervading, unbroken Consciousness - the reality and ground of all phenomena, which, according to the Advaita, consist of name and appearance only. This reality, existence, bliss - all vague, abstract words striving to express the inexpressible - is the supreme spirit and it is established in the centre of man's being. His sole spiritual vocation is to discover it and to know his identity with it.

The great philosopher Shri Shankara is the supreme exponent of this school of thought, and in his commentary on the *Bhagavad Gita*, which is the principal scripture of India, he defines the word *Adhyatma* as that which first shows itself as the ego - the innermost self in the body - but which turns out to be identical with the supreme reality - God.

Adhyatma Yoga is based on a three-pronged

1

foundation - if this does not sound too uneasy a position to be maintained. First, it relies on logical and subtly conceived philosophical argument; secondly, on a process of training by which the sleeping capacity in man to know his true nature - to know reality - is awakened; and thirdly - and very important this - on the testimony and instruction which has been left by a great concourse of seers and sages, both male and female, stretching from the earliest times down to the present day, all of whom have reached this peak of existence.

The deep subtlety and logic which clothe the philosophical approach to this Yoga have very seldom been appreciated or acknowledged in the West. Investigators have followed the argument up to a certain point, but after that they relapse into accusations of pantheism, fatalism, escapism and, very often, atheism. But the Teachers of this Yoga have never avoided criticism. In fact they have always held that individual experiment and experience are essential for real understanding, and that unprejudiced investigation should be carried out from the very first. They have left many invaluable works to guide the pupil in his researches. After all, if the contentions of the Advaita are true, they will eventually find confirmation in other fields, in the scientific and psychological fields for instance, and this has already begun to take place.

But the philosophical aspect of this Yoga is only one of its riches. Its second asset is the training it guards and offers to those who are ready for it. Control and equanimity of the mind is the principal technique taught by this discipline, for this is the necessary condition preceding the awakening of the higher intuition which can recognise the Truth instantaneously and directly.

Intuition has a very bad name in this part of the world today. Hitler is supposed to have used it and so too have many other now discredited people. But in fact all they developed was a subtle method of getting their own way, based on reasoning and their acquisitive faculties. The power of intuition and inspiration, on the other hand, acts instantaneously and inevitably and from its own centre, and it manifests unchanged by preferences and prejudices of the mind. In fact, it only awakens and operates after the mind has ceased to act as a guiding, influencing force.

Words such as these are notions that need a good deal of explanation, but the subject here is confined to the preliminary training, the preparation for Yoga, so I must put myself in the place of an enquirer and speak for him. What is the first thing such a one would want to know? He will surely ask why there is any necessity for training at all, or for restriction - for the word 'control' hints at it - if divinity and omniscience is the birthright of man, his natural state.

The answer to this is that, not only are we living most unnatural lives, but only a fraction of our powers are brought into play in the process. Those powers which are in evidence and are the property of the mind, such as the power of perception, reasoning, memory and so on, are usually in a state of instability and continuous activity. It is stated again and again in the Yoga classics and in the traditional instructions passed from Guru to pupil, that the universal and inexhaustible Power lies dormant behind this busy state of the mind and, when called forth, it can destroy fear and make a man a god and completely satisfied. But this Power will not be brought into operation until a sustained atmosphere of quiet and security and also a state of complete harmlessness have been established in the mind; then alone will this imperishable Truth reveal itself.

It is surely worth undergoing the discipline if only to test the truth of such a claim. But most people have already passed through some kind of training in their lives and do not enter another too easily. They know that it will demand patience, courage and enthusiasm, and also impose temporary restrictions upon them. During training every reaction seems to be out of proportion. Even conscious living, which simply means living with a sense of direction, does not appear to be a stable thing at all. It becomes *self*-conscious living, and the mind which you are trying to bring into focus perhaps for the first time, reveals itself as a whirlpool of instincts and resistances. But this is only natural, for when you decide to become the master of anything - to control it - you must be willing to experience its strengths and weaknesses, vicariously so to say, while you are bringing it into focus, and you will receive many surprises in the process.

Most of those born before World War II have at some time or other miserably gyrated round a room in the arms of a dancing mistress while she counted: 'One, two, three - reverse'. At that time dancing meant to us great misery, embarrassment and ceaseless vigilance and counting. But later it became for some at any rate a living and creative art, an interpretation of musical themes. Dancing is a specialised art practised by few only, but every man who is born into the world comes into it with latent powers awaiting development. Moreover, unless they are awakened and brought into focus, he will die half a man, ignorant of the greatness which lies within him and yet subconsciously aware of some deficiency of experience which was his right. We shall never know whether the claims made by those who would teach us about our inner nature are based on fact or fiction unless we patiently investigate, enquire, and risk the hardships of a training.

Let us suppose that the investigator says: 'Granted that this supra-mental power does exist, how am I to know that it exists in me in anything but a rudimentary form? In other words, how am I to know that it exists universally, as is claimed, and not in isolated beings only?' The answer to this is that it may be inferred from the testimony of those who have already awakened this power in themselves. They affirm that in this state they become directly aware of the inter-penetration by Consciousness, not of their own being alone, but of the whole phenomenal field also, just as the ether is interpenetrated by solar rays. And furthermore, no matter how high and into what abstract regions their awareness rises, they feel centred, that is - at home - and in their natural state. Like Peter and John, who were present at the transfiguration of the Lord Jesus, they feel instinct-ively: 'It is good for us to be here.'

Only personal experiment and experience can establish the truth of such a statement, for the means through which this knowledge is achieved is extremely personal. It is attained through the practice of meditation and contemplation. Meditation and con-templation! Now at last the investigator thinks he is on firm ground, for he feels that at least he knows his capacities in this direction and he is convinced that meditation will always remain a closed book to him. He assures you that he could never keep his mind on a meditation for two minutes; he is quite sure of that.

And yet this very man is capable of sitting with unseeing eyes in a bus, meditating in his mind on the re-arrangement of his house and furniture so that the new television set may be adequately housed. This meditation may go on for ten minutes or longer, during which time he is utterly oblivious to sights, sounds and physical contacts. What is this but meditation? It may not be a very high meditation on an abstract theme, but it is sustained. Why, the man is a born meditator!

A woman will tell you that she can't visualise anything, that she must have it before her eyes before she can call it to mind. 'When I was a child I couldn't visualise the map of England, I could never put in the capes and bays on the east coast. I know I could never practise contemplation.' Yet she can go into a brown study and sketch in her mind the features of someone she loves, and do it with joy and accuracy, or she can equally easily scratch in the defects of one she does not love, in pitiless detail. She is surely a contemplative in the making, though still unaware of her powers. There must be something which is lacking or is very weak in spiritual meditations, which is alive and strong in the self-imposed meditations of these two people.

There must be something which makes the one a theoretical exercise and the other almost a hidden vice. What is this mysterious quality? It is *identification*. Identification is the root from which springs devotion, worship and love.

My Teacher, Dr Shastri, used to say that love and worship must be learnt and practised like any other art, and that this was a vital part of the spiritual training. It is true that the mind is secretly selective and retentive, but it is also true that it can be coloured by images imposed upon it. Therefore the pupil is taught to train

6

his mind consciously by placing before it those concepts which will expand and make it lighter. This is one of the laws behind the repetition of the mantram or of the seed word such as OM. Descriptions of the lives of the great saints or of an Incarnation of God, or even a conception of an abstract truth, if dwelt upon in mental relaxation, can arouse the imagination and awaken this sense of identification, and then the quality of life will be changed for ever.

Once in ancient times, a certain king of Delhi, King Jalaluddin, caught a parrot. It was a sweet-speaking parrot but it had only one theme - the beauty and perfections of its mistress, the Rajput princess, Princess Padmini. It had strayed away from her palace in the great Fort of Chitor and had lost its way, never to find it again. Day after day the king listened half consciously to this paeon of praise from the parrot, until slowly his imagination was fired and he became obsessed with the desire to possess her. He raised an army and marched against the great Fort of Chitor, the stronghold of the Rajputs, and demanded that they should hand over the princess to him. But these warriors refused to surrender her, for they were a high-souled people and they knew that this life has no value whatsoever if it cannot protect truth and virtue. So the siege began, and in one day alone the Rajputs lost twenty thousand warriors, and four young princes were anointed kings one after another on the battlements, only to lose their lives in the fighting. At last a breach was made in the great walls and King Jalaluddin rode into the Fort at the head of the forces. He found that all the defenders had perished, and the women, with the Princess Padmini at their head, had joined them and jumped into the flames.

The whole situation sprang from the transformation of the heart of a great king as a result of listening to the reiterated laments of a parrot. The seeker after liberation also hears the description of spiritual beauty uttered again and again by the Teachers. He reads their inspired words. And if he listens and reads with open eyes and ears, without defences or prejudices, the desire for the hidden treasure can awaken in his heart. This is why the Teachers recommend *shravana* and *manana* - listening and reflecting - as the first steps to be taken on the spiritual journey.

But after interest has been aroused in this way, it must be fanned into something more urgent and intense. It must pass from enquiry to identification. The inner and outer discipline - the inner practice of meditation and the outer practice of a dedicated life and consciously directed action - are taught at this stage, because through them the flame of identification may be kindled and Truth pass from hearsay to reality. The point at which a pupil ceases to admire with his mind, crying out: 'How beautiful, how wonderful' and begins to whisper in his heart: 'I must possess this thing', is a turning point in his inner career, as it was in the worldly life of King Jalaluddin.

How do the Teachers pass on the secrets of the outer training - the discipline of conscious living and action - to their pupils? Traditionally the Adhyatma Yogis are participators in life and workers among men. They live lives of controlled and specialised action, which bear a resemblance to the life of a pilgrim - or a mountaineer, if you prefer it. The only reason why the mountaineer is where he is - often in a perilous position on a narrow ledge - is in order that he may carry out his project, namely to reach the summit and help his fellow climbers to reach it too. Every happening, his health, the general conditions, his food, his moods, are judged by him simply and solely on whether they help or hinder his design. He harbours his strength in order to go further, he restricts his food in order to become harder, and he expends his energy like a miser pays out gold. Of course these remarks apply to the climber and not to the one who has arrived. He can expend his energy as he likes and do what he likes, for he is beyond injunctions and prohibitions.

A pupil who has taken the decision to attempt the spiritual climb will also have to work according to a plan. He too will have to judge his instruments, that is, his mind and body, in just the same way that the mountaineer does, namely, in relation to whether they help or hinder him in gaining his end. It is the mind on which the training is concentrated in this Yoga, and the pupil is constantly warned that it can be his best friend or his most dangerous enemy. This may seem strange to us, for in the West the mind is associated with the thinking principle. But in the East the word *antah-karana* - mind - covers the entire composite inner instrument: the will, the ego, the faculty of perception and conception, the thinking principle, the discrim- inative faculty, in fact all that makes man a man, empirically speaking. In these last words lies the crux of the whole matter. The mind, if allowed free rein, will not only make man, man, but it will also keep man, man. He has identified himself with its activities for so long that he thinks he is the mind.

On the principle that it is always easier to deal in a detached way with other people's troubles than with your own, the first item of training is to disentangle and disidentify yourself from your mind, to look on it as if

9

it were your pupil, and then to direct it from a distance. In order to achieve this disidentification, you must affirm again and again, until it becomes a sort of mantram to you, that you are not the body, that you are not the mind, but that you are superior to them - that you are the supreme spirit. Having reiterated this for some time, you change the affirmation to: 'The mind is my instrument. I, the supreme Power, can and will control it.' Having spent some time on this, and only you will know how long it should be, you start the next practice, which is carrying out what you have affirmed - the controlling of this instrument.

It is inevitable that these practices will appear baby-easy at first, but it is also inevitable that most people will find them quite enough to employ them for some time. To control the mind you must learn to start it, steer it and stop it, as if it were a car. The aim of this trio of practices - starting, steering and stopping - is to bring the mind into focus as an object, and then to teach it to obey your orders. If you do not become at any rate partially successful in these preliminary practices, your later experiences in meditation and conscious living will somewhat resemble surf-bathing or being on the witching waves at a fair.

You can do the exercises given at any time. In fact, it is almost better to do them in the day, during your working life, than when shut up by yourself in your room. For instance, as you are sitting in the train, going to work and reading the daily paper, give your mind the order: 'Stop!', and instantaneously cease reading, and not only cease reading, but make your mind cease to think of what it has been reading. Hold it in suspension for a minute and then start it again on an entirely different theme.

It doesn't matter at this stage whether the subject you now present it with is secular or spiritual. The purpose of the practice is to teach your mind obedience. Say you decide to think for five minutes about your summer holiday, or about your coming work during the day, or about the meaning of a sentence you read earlier in a spiritual classic - it is all one. Let the mind carry out the order and then stop it again when the time limit has been reached. In this way you are practising starting, steering and stopping the mind.

These practices must seem almost inane and certainly very restricting, but they will not have to be used for long. After a certain time, varying with each pupil, the mind will have learnt to obey a percentage, at any rate, of your orders, or alternatively, you will be aware of its disobedience. In either case you will have brought your mind into focus. These practices should never be persisted in for very long at a time. The mind must be given frequent rests. The control will become automatic in due course, as the dancing steps became automatic after the agony of the first lesson was over.

This control lays the foundation on which meditation and consciously directed action are based. Control is imperative, for a mind which is capable of sustained concentration only when it is interested, and which refuses to apply itself to anything which is foreign and distasteful to it, will be of no use to you when you get to the higher reaches of Yoga.

Practise moderation: that is, get to know how long you can stand these exercises before you get tired of them and dismiss them as no good. Great things very often start in small ways, and if you persevere with these suggestions, you will have cause to be thankful all your yogic life.

II

THE POWER BEHIND THE MIND

ONLY AN illumined man can have direct knowledge of
spirit or Consciousness - the Power behind the mind.
In a manner of speaking, any power which goes against
the instinctive nature of the mind may be said to be a
higher power of that mind. In this sense, concentration
can certainly be said to be a higher power, for it is
infinitely superior in quality to the diffused unselective
activity which is the natural characteristic of the
untrained mind. To speak more correctly, however,
the mind does not possess any higher powers in its own
right, for just as the peak of a high mountain is the first
to flush with the light of the rising sun but is not a light
itself, so the highest peak of the mind, the apex, the
function known in Sanskrit as *buddhi*, or the faculty of
direct spiritual perception and pure intuition, is the
first to catch the light of the rising sun of
Consciousness, but it sheds no light of itself.

The destiny of the mind is not to be enriched and
loaded with powers but to be unloaded and absorbed
into the great Power which stands behind and within it
- the power of Consciousness. It is true that the mind is
subject to transformation, but when the state of
transcendence is reached it is no longer active.
Wonderful things may be performed through it, but not
by it.

Just as a safe containing great treasure only opens to
what is known as a 'special combination', so that
highest function of the mind known as *buddhi*, which

12

hides the treasure, does not yield it up until a special combination has been applied. A *thirst for release, devotion and continuity of purpose* form that combination, and, since God is not mocked, it never works on a pseudo-application. We shall only have access to that part of the mind-safe where the less valuable treasures are lodged, until we learn to use the full combination.

Many achieve worldly success through concentration born of will directed to a special empirical end, but the higher Power cannot be so used by man, nor is it the property of his mind. That Power uses his mind and his whole organism for its own higher and cosmic purposes, but it will not become operative until the mind has become its instrument and has been laid down empty before it. This is the object of all spiritual discipline and austerity - the laying down of one form of activity and the taking up of another and a higher.

What is the conception of consciousness in the West? Awareness - awareness of something, awareness which lies inherent in the mind but which needs the co-operation of the mind and the sense-organs before it can function. Consciousness is thus perception - either mental or sensory - and is a distinctive characteristic of the mind. The idea that Consciousness could exist independently of a ground for its manifestation, is neither acceptable nor even seriously considered here as yet.

According to the Eastern teaching, Consciousness is not the property of anything nor does it completely reside in any object. All objects reside in it, like islands in a sea. Matter, force and mind are its evolutes and its dependants. It is the great independent root, the motionless medium for all activity. Empirical consciousness is but a partial manifestation of that greater

Consciousness. There is nothing outside or independent of it; nothing exists but by its permission. Everything is Consciousness in varying degrees of opaqueness or illumination. It is called chit in Sanskrit and it is one of the triple designations of God: *sat chit ananda* - meaning existence absolute, consciousness absolute, and bliss absolute. These three aspects are only partially known to man while he works empirically, but they are present everywhere and all the time, to be experienced in their fullness by whoever is willing to pay the price for so doing.

It will be seen that these two definitions of Consciousness - the one 'awareness' and the other 'spirit' - differ widely and essentially from one another. Although Western thought today is reducing all matter and energy to one category, and is giving both energy and matter a common root, it is not envisaged that that root is Consciousness. The implications of these two attitudes are most important and need to be appreciated if an understanding of the significance of the Advaita philosophy - the philosophy of non-duality, upon which this Yoga is based - is to be attempted.

Now for the mind. According to the West, the mental apparatus is a reservoir or inland sea of instinctive, blind forces. Freud postulated this reservoir, made up of forces from which and upon which the personality is built up. As the mind grows - and the meaning of 'grows' here is 'becomes more aware of the forces around it' - it learns to exercise increasing control over them and to harness them to its own purposes, good or bad. The ego is, so to say, a little island in this sea of unconscious, primitive forces, and is made up of refined mind-stuff, self-aware, and with the power to censor the impulses coming up from that sea - to repress or give rein to them. If repressed, these mental forces are only checked and not destroyed, and if no outlet is given to them they vent themselves by weakening the foundations of the personality from within; for a force dammed up and not diverted is destructive. The point to notice here is that the phrase 'growth of the mind' involves an increasing awareness and an ability to deal with mental and physical phenomena, but no more.

Freud says that the contents of the unconscious determine the life of the mind. The East not only says the same thing, but also says that this can be changed, and it has a highly developed technique for doing so. It teaches that if a man is to become willing - or to put it more strongly, if a man is to feel impelled - to control the instincts of selfishness and ego-preservation and to undergo the rigours of discipline in order to do so, he must be given something greater than the ego on which to fix his heart and mind. According to Vedanta, this focus, which is chosen for him by the Teacher, is at first a concrete object, or form, but as the man advances and matures he is given a focus which is more abstract and universal. Finally, the concept of his real Self, the spiritual element in him - chit or Consciousness - is brought before him and claims his complete attention and allegiance.

According to Vedanta, Consciousness is sleeping in the rocks and stones, stirring in the plants and animals, half-awakened in the ordinary man and fully awakened in the God-realised saint. This is what Vedanta means by evolution. The ego is guided from the primitive, veiled consciousness of inanimate matter, through all the stages of life, until it eventually realises its true

nature as it is, and always has been. This last stage of
the journey is made consciously and with effort, and is
the culmination of the half-conscious struggle against
limitations which has accompanied the whole development. Why does the ego press forward towards the
Light? Why doesn't it go round and round in a circle?
There is an original impetus, free and not determined,
at the root of phenomena and in the condition of things
- an impetus in them to change, evolve and to manifest
and experience their inmost nature, which is divine.

In Vedanta, the mind is conceived as the entire inner
organ of man and is called the *antahkarana*. It consists
of *manas* - the lower mind, the unselective, recording
function; *chitta* - the emotions, will and memory; the
lower *buddhi* - the empirical reason, and the higher
buddhi, which is the intuitive, spiritual faculty; and
finally the Lord High Executioner himself - the ego -
ahankara.

Now, unlike the West, where the problem is to
control and manipulate forces for the benefit and
enrichment of the mind, the problem here is the
unveiling of the one great force of Consciousness, in
order that it may function untrammelled by the
limitation of any medium, although capable of using
any medium for its purpose.

In this sense the mind may be thought of as a star in
the firmament of Consciousness. While it is still dark
(while Consciousness is still veiled and confined and
ignorance prevails), the star diffuses light. But when
the sun of Consciousness rises, the mind-star fades into
insignificance before that superior Light and, although
still in the sky, it is no longer seen and ceases to be a
purveyor of light.

People may perhaps think here: 'It is all very well to

16

deal so arbitrarily with the mind as a whole and to dissolve it so satisfactorily to yourself, but what about my ego? As long as I live, I shall have that to deal with, I suppose?' The more you think about the ego, even about killing or dissolving it, the worse it will become and the more unmanageable. Like the *enfant terrible*, the more you try to control and cajole it, the more it will show off. What can be done?

In order to become detached from anything, you must convince yourself that you can obtain greater satisfaction from something else. Otherwise your efforts will lead to suppression, which is imprisonment, and not detachment, which is liberty. Therefore the best thing to do is to have an interest superior to it - 'metal more attractive'. A thirst for release, a desire for real understanding of the truths taught in the philosophy, the schooling of the heart in devotion, all represent these stronger and higher interests. They will put the ego out of focus, very satisfactorily, in time.

The ego is a point of stress; it is the centre of a whirlpool of power in a sea of Consciousness. A whirlpool is water in a sea of water, and only receives a form by virtue of its own impetus, which restricts it to that shape. So the ego of man is the centre of a whirlpool of Consciousness in a sea of Consciousness, restricted to a form by virtue of the impetus generated by past *karma* - desires, memories and so forth. The task is to resolve this whirlpool back into water, in other words, to expand the limited consciousness back into that Consciousness which is God, and which contains both the limited and the infinite, and to whom all things are alike and equally good.

In order to uncover the higher power, the mind need not be killed. But it must be restrained from unselective activity, expanded and absorbed. The process by which we bring about this transformation is the discipline laid down in all spiritual schools: meditation, purification, control and research into the philosophical basis of the Truth. If this discipline is faithfully carried out, the result will be that the centre of gravity will pass, so to say, from the mind to Consciousness itself. But just as no meal can be cooked without a fire, however delicious and carefully prepared the ingredients may be, so the spiritual awakening will not come to pass without the fire of love of God having been lit in the heart and without His grace.

Why does the process of meditation, purification and control have a transforming effect on the mind? In his book on meditation, *Meditation - Its Theory and Practice*, Dr Shastri says that meditation does not create perfection, but it allows perfection to reveal itself by removing the obstacles to its realisation. In other words, meditation isolates, restrains and quietens the mind, thereby bringing out its latent capacity for spiritual absorption.

Purification involves the elimination from the mind of anything which is not of good repute, and the relinquishment of those things which will hamper its ability to carry out its spiritual duty and destiny. This one-pointedness of the mind is not the matter of an hour or of a day, but of the whole life. It produces in the mind the mood of non-attachment. Non-attachment is another name for the death of preferences. The death of preferences will release the mind from the fetters of incarnations of emotional ties, and make it worthy to be called an instrument and not an impediment.

Control produces concentration. In fact, in the

spiritual life they are synonymous, or rather, one is
never present without the other. Our Teacher says that
the secret and basis of concentration, on which so
much depends, is a good and dedicated life. This may
seem rather an anti-climax when one has visualised it as
an all-in wrestling match with the mind at the time of
meditation - but there it is. If the life is not consciously
directed, if the mind is full of desires, anger, loves and
hates, it will be mercurial and keep you for ever tossing
this way and that in suspense. Like Atalanta, you will
stop in your race to pick up many a golden apple, and
so lose the greater prize. A good life, according to
Yoga, is a life where self-interest is no interest at all,
and where devotion to God, to Truth and the service of
all living beings, are the guiding principles. These are
harmonising, quietening principles, which, by restr-
aining the fluctuations of the mind, prepare it for its
transit from individuality to universality. Such perfection may be beyond our reach at present, but still - this
is the teaching.

This technique is given with slight variations in many
classics, but there is one passage from the *Maitri
Upanishad* which states it very clearly:

> Having settled down (having made his choice), let
> him, being pure himself and pure in goodness,
> study the truth, speak the truth, think the truth and
> sacrifice for the truth. Henceforth he becomes
> another. His fetters are cut asunder; he knows no
> expectation, no fear from others, as little as from
> himself; he knows no desires. Freedom from desire
> is, as it were, the highest prize to be taken from the
> best treasury. For a man full of desires, being
> possessed of will, imaginings and self-conceit, is a

slave, but he who is the opposite is free. For this reason let the man stand free from will, imaginings and self-conceit. This is the sign of liberty, this is the path that leads to God, this is the opening of the door, and through it he will go to the other shore beyond darkness, for therein all desires are contained. When the five instruments of knowledge (the senses) stand still, together with the mind, and when the intellect does not move, that is called the highest state.

The three things that the Sage says must be given up are will, imaginings and self-conceit. The three traditional disciplines of meditation, purification and control, are the practices by which these attributes may be eliminated. They link up together. All these three - will, imaginings and self-conceit - have to do with the individualised mind and they all form a successful barrier to its final expansion. The term 'will' as used in this Upanishad means the will born of desire - the determination to carry out imaginings which have been aroused by latent desires produced by *karma* (the impressions left by past actions).

In the Gita it is written: 'No-one becomes a yogi who has not relinquished *sankalpa*.' *Sankalpa* is the picture-making, planning, desiring faculty. Springing from deep individual preferences and employing, as it does, nearly every mental and emotional activity, it successfully claims man's attention and vitality for incarnations. Spiritual discipline is directed towards the breaking down of this activity with its limited and self-directed sphere of action, so that, in the end, the whole being may be offered to God. It is normal and natural for man to make this offering, for that Power is his real Self. He is *sat-chit-ananda* - existence, consciousness and bliss. He is, in fact, only offering his limited self to his unlimited Self, and, when he has done so, he becomes omniscient and blissful.

For the man who has reached this goal of life, inspiration, direct cognition and the higher *samadhi* are his forever. The higher *samadhi* is a vision, an endless vision, for when it is once had it is never lost again. It is a subjective vision in which the inner eye sees reality *as it is*; and since one of the attributes of God or reality is bliss, when man recognises this reality as his own nature, he has perpetual bliss, a bliss surpassing anything which can be experienced on earth.

When he reaches this eminence, the man is endowed with direct perception of spiritual knowledge. The mind is now fully absorbed, functionless, empty, pure and still, the light of Consciousness alone shining. Under that light all is seen as it really is. The illumined man still acts, but he acts under the illumination of that Light, and not under the limited light of his individual mind. That mind is still there, like the star in the sunlit sky mentioned in the illustration, but it is not the purveyor of light. This is what is meant in the passage from the *Maitri Upanishad*: 'The five instruments of knowledge (the senses) stand still, together with the mind, and the intellect does not move.' When this takes place, it is called the highest state - *samadhi* - illumination.

You may be sure that the state just described would never be called the 'highest state' if it were a void, a vacuum or a nullity. It is so called because it is a fullness and a fulfilment, and this could only be so if there were something supremely conscious to fill that empty place. That apparent emptiness, in fact, contains fullness, and forms the ground for the play of the higher Power. This emptiness, which has necessarily been misunderstood in the West and has alarmed many, is seen to be the hub of the mental and spiritual universes when approached through the teachings of Vedanta.

The old Chinese philosopher Lao Tzu understood this doctrine well, and he has written:

> Thirty spokes surround one nave,
> The usefulness of the wheel is always in that
>   empty innermost.
> You fashion clay to make a bowl,
> The usefulness of the bowl is always in that
>   empty innermost.
> You cut out doors and windows to make a
>   house,
> Their usefulness to the house is always in their
>   empty space.
> Therefore 'profit' comes from external form,
> But 'usefulness' from the empty innermost.

The word 'profit' here means empirical enrichment. 'Usefulness' means the ability to fulfil that for which the thing was made; in the case of man - omniscience.

III

RENUNCIATION - THE WAY TO FREEDOM

THE SUBJECT of this talk is how to become free - that
is, how to know yourself to be fearless, unassailable,
completed - and capable of passing strength and hope to
others. I am told that the title: 'Renunciation - the
Way to Freedom', reeks of restriction and asceticism,
and that it is sure to antagonise many, who will say:
'Well, if Yoga is based on this sort of training, it is no
better than the rigorous Christian discipline of the
Middle Ages, and it will certainly be of no use to me!'
Now I don't believe this, for although, until it is
understood, the word 'renunciation' may have a dying
fall, the word 'freedom' is like the morning itself,
which drowns darkness in light and is alive and
progressive. Surely, anything which may lead to that
state of things is worth investigating.

One of the gifts this Yoga can give to those who
follow it, is the knowledge that all men are in essence
divine, and this implies that they have always been
divine and will never cease to be so. The picture man
usually presents of varying degrees of domination or
inefficiency is the result of ignorance. This is not the
negative ignorance of not knowing through the mind. It
is a primal ignorance, or nescience, which is positive
and a divine instrument, for through its power,
creation - the conception of multiplicity - comes into
play, the world swims into view and the eternal non-
dual reality appears as seeming multiplicity, limited by
attributes.

In the outer world this multiplicity manifests as names and forms, colours and gradations of vitality. In the inner world, the world of man's subjective being, it manifests as the mind, the senses, the emotions, the memory and the vital force. The unbroken play of this primal nescience forms the basic root of the world and produces the alternations of pleasure and pain, hate and love, in fact all the attractions and repulsions which make up the phenomenon called in Sanskrit *sansara*, or that moving thing, the world.

As far as man is concerned, the instrument which introduces him into this turmoil of existence and keeps him there, is the mind - itself the most important detail in the magic show. According to the Vedanta philosophy, the mind, or *antahkarana*, means the inner organ of activity as against the outer organ of the body, and it is a recording, hoarding, testing machine. The major activity of most people during their lives is to receive through the mind, and pack away in it, impressions, fears and desires. They have identified themselves with these things, and are therefore ruled by them unknowingly. Such impressions, fears and desires colour their relationships with the outer world, until the spiritual science has been learnt by which they can be neutralised.

The supreme reality cannot be described in the language of men; it can only be indicated and in relative terms. It is unchangeable and interpenetrates undetected the whole creation - before, behind, above, below and within. These words are themselves a product of *maya* or the agent of multiplicity; nevertheless they give a picture by which the Whole may be theoretically apprehended by the imagined part.

In the realm of *maya*, the supreme reality is

24

conceived as Consciousness, which, ever the same in itself, manifests in varying degrees in the thousands of forms which constitute the empirical world. Thus Consciousness is said to be progressively manifest in matter, flora, fauna and human beings. It is recognised by man as being the self-consciousness within him, and is known in its fullness by the spiritually illumined sages only.

This is another way of saying that reality - or what is called the Self, partless and supremely independent of all phenomena, the only lasting principle - is ever-present, to be revealed in due time within the awakened man, who will recognise it as his fundamental nature. This is true, but it is only after 'he has risen from his mound of dust, has ordered his life and has looked upon the Sun', that he will know it to be truth and will be transformed by this knowledge. Until then, the spiritual Sun will be concealed and overlaid by phenomena, in other words by the mind, for this power - called maya - which splits unity into diversity, operates wherever the mind can reach. It promotes multiplicity, and its accomplice, the mind, recognises and savours it.

But all the while, interpenetrating both maya and the mind, above, below and within, lies the supreme spirit, ever the same and self-luminous, which implies that its light and nature is derived from itself alone, and from no independent source. All spiritual training, whether yogic or otherwise, has for its aim the withdrawal of the mental or mayic activity to the background in order that this divine power may manifest, be brought to the foreground, and finally dominate the scene.

You may say: 'If this spirit is supreme and

unassailable, as you maintain, how can it possibly be overcome and distorted by a lesser power - this power called *maya*?' The answer is that it is neither overcome nor distorted nor made less, for it is ever untouched. The Self, the supreme reality, is not changed or acted upon by the clouds which temporarily obscure it. It will shine out again in its original brilliance, when the clouds have dissipated.

The supreme Self is revealed through the action of powers which lie beyond or above the mind, and they only become active as the result of discipline and training. Just as scientific instruments can extend the range of the physical senses and enable them to view hitherto unknown objects, so these inner and higher faculties can be concentrated, controlled and extended by traditional practices and training, and in this way the omnipotent Power can be directly known. This assertion is neither hearsay nor personal opinion, but the testimony of illumined sages of the past *and* the present - for some of them are with us even today.

Now the seeker will probably have another question to ask and it is: 'Why has this cosmic tangle taken place at all? Why must there be this interplay of beauty and horror, of joy and grief?' In Dr Shastri's book, *World Within the Mind*, which was translated from the great classic, *Yoga Vasishtha*, the pupil, Prince Rama, asks this very question of his Guru, the sage Shri Vasishtha. He says:

Tell me, O high-minded Sage, how could creation proceed from the supreme *Brahman* (which is the Sanskrit name for God, the Absolute) whom you represent as motionless in the void? Anything which is produced from something is invariably of the same nature as its producer. Light is produced from light; corn from corn; man is born of man. Therefore that which is created by the immutable spirit must itself be unchangeable and spiritual by nature. Besides, the intelligent spirit of God is pure and immaculate, whilst all creation is impure and of gross matter.

On hearing these words, the great Sage said:

O Ramaji, *Brahman* is all purity and there is no impurity in Him. The waves moving on the surface of the ocean may be foul, but they do not soil the waters of the deep.

Prince Rama rejoined:

Sir, your discourse is very abstruse and I cannot understand the meaning of what you say. *Brahman* is devoid of sorrow, while the world is full of sorrow. I cannot therefore understand you when you say that this is the offspring of That.

The great Sage remained silent at the words of Prince Rama. He thought: 'It is no fault of the educated if they are doubtful of something until it has been explained to them to their satisfaction, as in the case of Prince Rama. The pupil has first to be prepared and purified through meditation, devotion and the service of Yoga and by the daily practice of tranquillity and self-control, and then slowly initiated into the conviction that all is *Brahman*.' Then he said:

O Rama, at the conclusion of these discourses I

will tell you whether the dross of gross bodies is attributable to *Brahman* or not. For the present, know that *Brahman* is almighty, all-pervading and is Himself all, in the same sense that a magician produces many things which are unreal appearances in the sight of man.

So Prince Rama is told here that knowledge only comes through inner maturity which is attained by discipline and spiritual application, and never through book-learning alone. There are many such discussions between the Teacher and the disciple in this work and the whole book is full of beauty and teaching.

Dr Shastri once said that the questions 'why?' and 'how?' and the speculations as to the reason for suffering, wars, illness, torture and the like, arise on the plane of *maya* and will never be solved on that plane. Man must rouse himself and pass from self-consciousness to universal consciousness if he is to understand the mystery of the trinity: the unconscious, the self-conscious and the supra-conscious. So the answer seems to be that the part can never know the whole and that we, imagined parts, will only know in truth when we know ourselves to be the Whole. This is the purpose of the Yoga training and it is also the goal of life.

What is the process through which man rouses himself, and then passes from the mayic to the eternal state - from the sense of separation and of being a part, to knowing himself to be the Whole? This transformation is said to be brought about through renunciation. What is true renunciation and what are we to renounce? Above all, why is renunciation capable of producing such inner changes?

This renunciation is traditionally held to be essential before growth can take place. It is in fact synonymous with transcendence, a word with much wider and more vital implications than renunciation. To the majority of men, growth means expansion, acquisition of wider scope, knowledge and possessions. But to the spiritual investigator, growth signifies transcendence, the progress from a search for increasing detail about an object or concept, to intuitive knowledge of that thing through detachment, purity and concentration.

The value and significance of an object or concept always exceeds any empirical knowledge of it, for it will never be truly known through an assessment of its component parts. Voltaire has said that a man could have a thousand senses and yet come no nearer to knowing the eternal than a man with five. True knowledge is not gained by the piling up of data, but by the submersion of the mind in the object to be known. This feat is brought about by meditation and contemplation, the bridge over which all men will pass on their way from the temporal and unreal to the real.

But what is the significance of transcendence, and how does it lead to freedom? Although it may not appear to be a fact, it is a fundamental characteristic of man's nature to seek universality. He wants everything and will always want it. At first he wants everything for himself. Later he wants everything for all. Finally, his understanding of the term 'everything' undergoes a radical change, and it is at this point that he transcends the mind and goes free. He is also antipathetic to 'narrowness', which he interprets at first as restriction - restriction of his personal scope and mental range - but which he later realises to be due to the action of his lower self, his ego.

Ego! Now that the word has appeared and the cosmic cat is out of the bag, we had better assign it its place in the drama. Ego, the sense of self-reference, the 'I' sense, is held to be the chief enemy of man, the brake on his wheel, so to say. Its throne is the mind, which is itself the field on which the battle for liberation and conscious immortality will be fought out. You cannot overcome *maya*, or the sense of individualisation, by action taken in the objective world; it can only be dealt with on the mental plane.

A writer has said that the ego is man's mistress in a wondrous love-affair which unfortunately is apt to outlast all the others, and that she can keep him dancing attendance on her, striving to please her whims, for incarnations. According to our Teacher, however, the reason why the ego exercises such power over man, both for attraction and the opposite, is because it has a dual action, or nature. On the one hand it can identify itself with the mind and the body, cleaving to the world and all that therein is. But in its higher aspect, the ego harbours a ray of the supreme Consciousness which is ever unaffected by these things, and it can be illumined by that divine ray. This is why man in his heart of hearts thinks, and in fact he is right so to think: 'I am great - I am greater than you know'. He thinks this even while he is striving to free himself from the octopus-like clutches of his lower self. But knowledge, as always, will come to the rescue here; for once he has realised the dual nature of this ego, he can use its higher aspect to overcome the lower.

According to the Yoga teaching, when you consider an object or a concept, you are joined to that object by a subtle bond. This subtle bond is the ego sense. It is the lower form of identification which ties man to objects, and its power of restriction must be recognised and transcended before man can become free. We say 'recognised' because unless he recognises the presence of restriction, and the desirability of escape from it, his impulse to escape will not be permanent.

A hundred years ago people used to travel by horses and carts - now they travel by air. They did not renounce horses and carriages because it was a good discipline to do so: they renounced them because they had found something quicker and less restricting. Therefore there was no danger of a return to the old method of locomotion. So it is with the instinct towards transcendence. Before the assault on the ego can succeed, we must be sure that we are heading for some state which is superior and permanently more desirable than our present one.

Now the question arises: 'How, in our ignorance, can we be certain of this?' It is at this point that, if he is to advance further, the investigator will have to become a pupil and undergo training. This is a serious step and will call every faculty he possesses into play. The idea of the necessity for training for the spiritual life is foreign to the West, except in the case of specialists such as priests and nuns, and not only is it foreign but it is usually regarded as rather excessive and unnecessary.

No-one minds being specially trained in, say, the science of hydraulics; in fact one would expect to undergo a stiff course of instruction because no ordinary person could be expected to have any idea of such a subject. But when it comes to living as a spiritual man, knowing how to think and what to think and how to promote growth in the spiritual sense, it is a different matter. Everyone is supposed to know this science instinctively - which is nonsense. The only fact that man knows instinctively, while he is struggling with his mind and senses, is the mighty power of his *vasanas*, or sub-conscious promptings, which are for ever producing fresh attractions and restrictions to chain him down.

If he is to win freedom, he will not only have to be open to instruction, but he will also have to make his own contribution to spiritual eminence in the form of reverence and obedience. In all the Eastern schools the final goal of the training is the same - freedom through direct experience of Truth. But before that final goal can be realised, which means, before the transform-ation of the individual man into a universal being can be effected, he has to pass from revelation to revelation, through the acceptance of certain basic facts. For example, here are two preliminary and yet fundamental ones which a pupil must accept and act upon if he is to go further.

It is a universal teaching imparted by all Gurus of both East and West, though in different ways, that the imperishable Truth can only be revealed in a quiescent mind. A quiescent mind is a mind which allows objects or concepts to come into it and dissolve in it, instead of going out to these things and becoming dissipated in them.

The second basic fact is not so universally taught, but it is a cardinal point of this Yoga. It is held that the imperishable Truth can only be understood by a heart which has recognised the unity of life and which sees the whole creation as based on the one spirit and interpenetrated by it. Our Teacher has said that man is connected with every plant and every star and that his thoughts affect the whole universe. This truth of the universality of Consciousness must at any rate be accepted in theory before the way will be open to advance further.

The pupil is confronted with these two facts from the moment he starts his training. They are fundamental, and unless they are slowly and consciously accepted and their significance grasped, no meditation, service or study will develop to the full. Both these teachings deal blows to the ego and, if they are patiently carried out, will bring about its dethronement. The quiescent mind is anathema to the lower ego, which is like a bee, never satisfied with one flower, but for ever buzzing on after fresh scents. There are perfumes far more exquisite and rare than it has ever dreamed of, but unfortunately it cannot have access to them, nor would it appreciate them if it had. Nevertheless, the lower ego organises a strong resistance directly the pupil starts on the conscious practice of learning how to control and pacify his mind, and it spreads out the world in all its attractions before him in order to stay his progress. As for universality - where does the ego come in here? It is immediately on the alert, for it fears it will begin to lose its contour, like a ripple in water.

The pupil is expected to pay the agreed price in the currency of obedience and reverence. Reverence is that quality which makes it impossible for him to discount either the Teacher or his teachings. Obedience is the instantaneous acceptance of whatever comes. If the pupil pays this price, he will receive practices which will bring alive the two preliminary but essential inner states: the state of harmony, quiet and detachment, which is the state of good growing weather; and the state of recognition of the universal essence of Consciousness.

The dawning freedom thus acquired comes to the pupil through an intelligent acceptance. It is never gained through blind conformity, or excessive asceticism, or by renunciation for its own sake. Nor will it be completely won and the pupil freed, until he desires that state in every cell of his being. No need for him to fear that this climax will rush upon him and take him unawares, or half willing. It will probably be the other way about: he will be supremely willing long before it descends upon him.

For those who may wish to give Yoga a practical trial, here are two general practices. The first is for stilling the mind.

Sit either on the floor or upright but not rigid on a chair. Make a mental salutation either to an Incarnation of God or to the abstract all-pervading spirit, and breathe in and out for a few minutes, bringing in the breath as from the feet to the head and releasing it as from the head to the feet. Imagine that this breath has the power to dissolve all thought, as a light wind dissolves a mist. When you feel that the mind is still - or stiller than it was - cease the breathing and remain quiet yet alert for a short time. Then place one sentence in the mind and look at it and absorb it. You must choose your sentence before you start. It could well be one which will introduce you to your second practice which produces the sense of universality. For instance: 'All life is one', or: 'I was, I am, I shall be'. Spend five minutes or so in pondering over its meaning, then make another salutation and close the practice.

The second practice is the one which opens the heart to the universality of Consciousness or God and the consequent oneness of all. Sit still in the posture, but now your mind must be ready to receive thought. You say to it: 'I will not injure any by thought, word or deed. They are my Self', or: 'May no-one fear me and may I fear no-one', or: 'May all derive good from me, may I derive good from all'. Meditate on the thought for about five minutes. You will notice that each idea has two stages. 'May all derive good from me, and may I receive good from all', 'I forgive all, may all forgive me'. The second part of the thought is inserted to prevent the Lord of the Manor attitude from developing in the pupil! The sense of being a universal benefactor and the subtle satisfaction this produces spells a temporary victory for the ego and must be avoided at all costs, and this is a sure way to do it.

No doubt these practices will look as if they are very childish and easy, but this is not always found to be the case when they are tried out. You will only get to know how wiry your mind is when you try to quieten it and make it supple for even a few minutes. Many will only realise how much they dislike being forgiven or assisted when they use their imagination and their sense of humour to test their reactions in the second practice.

If the practices do begin to have a result, which should take the form of a sense of security, peace and expansion, then you can go forward into the practice of meditation with a hopeful heart. May this be so.

IV

THE THREE PATHS

THIS TALK is to be on the three paths of training, and its title implies that there is an objective to be reached on the spiritual journey. 'Surely this is obvious,' you will say, 'otherwise we should not be here.' But sometimes the impression is given that Yoga is a work-without-end affair, a perennial system of self-discipline and self-study, which is not only a full-time occupation but will last as long as we do. Someone has said that it is a good thing to be born in a religion, but a very bad thing to die in it. The meaning is that a philosophy or a belief is never an end in itself, for it must necessarily remain theoretical; it is merely a means to an end. This is doubly true about any Yoga through which the Truth is to be realised. The task is to bring the theory to life, to identify oneself, through the dethronement of egoity, with the affirmation of Truth which is made by the philosophy, and then to emerge on the other side of it, so to say, into the region where theory becomes reality - and furthermore, to do this before leaving this earthly life.

This point of view is more understandable in the East than it is here, where people expect to reach truth by deduction and reasoning alone and refuse to advance further than their minds can see and accept. The ancient sages of the East did not place so much faith in reasonable theories, so they did not necessarily discard them when they fell short of logical certainty. They looked on spiritual research as one of the functions in

36

the process of unveiling the supreme Truth. It was a move made in order to keep that Truth, which they had already intuitively grasped and accepted, in partial focus while they were training their higher faculties to realise it in its entirety.

The old philosophers of the East were seers, saints and trainers of saints. Their opinions were never personal: they were pronouncements made while in a transcendental state of consciousness. Therefore, with the exception of the materialistic school, their findings on the basic questions were in agreement. They all acknowledge the fact of the supreme Self or reality; their differences only arise in the lower reaches of thought. Here we tend to think that if a man is intelligent enough he can know everything. The Eastern belief is that only if man is pure enough can he really know anything. It is not until he has undergone a course of spiritual discipline and self-purification that the Truth will become real for him and bear fruit.

Now the *Advaita*, or teaching of non-dualism, has a universal character. It acknowledges one supreme reality, and holds that this reality animates all religions, forms the foundation of all phenomena and is the quickening force in every Incarnation of God, every saint, and every ordinary man. According to the teachings, there is only one supreme Consciousness, one power, one reality, which is not subject to growth and decay. It is present in its totality in all phenomena from an angelic being to a worm, from a star to a clod of earth. But it is partly concealed by nescience of varying densities, which is superimposed on it. In fact Consciousness revealing itself in individual forms is the root of the world.

Adhyatma Yoga, which trains those who are drawn

towards this vision of non-duality, is also a universal Yoga. The requirements of all grades of pupils are given equal consideration. The title of this talk speaks of three paths, but one path is not considered superior to another. The value of each approach lies in its training value to the disciple alone, and there are three main types of men who may wish to study this spiritual training.

There is a Japanese poem which says:

> Many paths there be
> To reach the mountain's height,
> But all who climb there see
> The same moon's light.

This conforms with the teaching of Yoga, and the three main avenues of approach may be roughly classified as: the path of action, the path of devotion, and the path of knowledge.

Most people, when they are brought face to face with something new, a new system of thought or a scientific discovery, will want to put it to the test, to see whether it works, how it works and whether they can work it. These are the practical enquirers who will walk the path of action. Then there are a smaller number who wish to take a new idea away and brood on it, in order to sense its atmosphere and possibilities intuitively and identify themselves with it. Later these are likely to be walkers on the path of devotion. Finally come those rare enquirers who have instinctive reverence and no prejudice for any system of thought they may encounter, but who will be receptive to what it has to offer and will postpone judgement until they have studied it. This is the perfect attitude for a pupil. At the start his sole object should be to fit himself to grasp the subject, rather than to try to fit the subject into a form acceptable to himself. He will learn nothing that way, but will only become more firmly ensconced in his own atmosphere.

Our Teacher used to tell us that there were three stages in the growing understanding of a disciple on the spiritual journey. During the initial stages he feels: 'I am His', which embodies the impulse towards service. He sees himself as a servant, an actor in the drama of the Lord, and a carrier-out of orders. He places his reasoning mind and his body at the disposal of God and his Teacher. In the second stage the disciple begins to awaken. A sense of the source from which he draws his strength and his orders is growing in him and he begins to feel his relationship with it. He now says: 'I am thine', meaning: 'I am in inner intuitive relationship with thee, O Lord, O Supreme!' This feeling, when held and fortified by the imagination, turns him into a devotee, one who places his emotions as well as his mind and body at the service of a Lord to whom he feels allied. The third stage is the culmination of training. Here the disciple does not say, but he knows: 'I am He'.

The disciple has now arrived within sight of his goal. He knows the Truth, if only theoretically. He has seen the mountain top even if he is still some distance away from it. In fact he is travelling the path of knowledge. The worship and service which before he offered to the personal God, or the Teacher, each being viewed as exterior to himself, are turned inwards and offered to the One without attributes, his own Self - which is the Self of all.

At the beginning of his training, the hearer will

inevitably be more influenced by one of these attitudes of mind than by the others. He will naturally be drawn at first either to experiment and put into practice, or to draw near and love, or to grasp by intuition and identification and to transcend. But his seeking mind and heart will not suffer itself to be neatly compressed on any one path or into any category for ever, and as he rises to maturity he seeks experience on each path in turn. It does not really matter to which approach he is drawn at first, provided he has a sense of direction, that is, an objective, and also a determination to reach that objective before the sands run out. This sense of the end in the beginning endows the whole training with life and movement, and is essential if the pupil is to keep his courage and enthusiasm alive and be able to meet the tests on his skill and endurance which will come by whatever path he travels.

When a traveller to the spiritual heights stands at the opening of his career, he will naturally desire to learn something of the technique of climbing, that is, what he must guard with his life and what he must throw away in order to lighten his load. An experienced fellow-traveller can advise him as to this, and he should turn to him if he is not to make too many mistakes. For instance, it is no use starting out in sand shoes just because one is going to cross the Gobi Desert, or to carry a television set up Mount Everest. We all know that the enthusiastic but short-lived dashes made by a hen after a morsel which has taken her fancy will never get her across the farmyard!

There are in fact three essential items of equipment which every spiritual climber must take with him: imagination, will and a trained capacity to form habits. This may seem a curious choice, but if these faculties are used in conjunction with one another and never by themselves, they will prove very present helps in time of trouble.

Habits are popularly supposed to be restrictive and deadening, but if you have ever tried to break one, you will realise that it also has a hidden and tenacious life and strength which can well be used to your advantage. It is a subtle form of habit which lies at the root of rhythm, continuity and harmony. Both recurrence and reiteration, which are based on the continuity of an idea, exercise great power over the mind. You have only to call to mind the advertisements you have succumbed to, merely because they have invaded your field of perception over and over again, to realise this. The practice of mantram is the habitual repetition of a sacred formula based on the hidden laws of rhythm and the directed action of spiritual force, and it is one of the most powerful of the Yoga practices.

Instinctive habits have little value, but a habit which was once consciously formed and has now become automatic, is a most powerful aid when you are dealing with anything as unpredictable as the mind. Mind training is really another name for habit-forming at the outset. If you have once trained your mind to stop automatically and to start again in a new direction, at an order, you have overcome one of the chief difficulties in the early stages of the practice of meditation.

There is an old story of two Buddhist monks who were one day walking in the country near their monastery. They were happy, arguing on high points of philosophy, but perhaps they were quite blind to the beauty of the country through which they were passing. Suddenly, coming round the shoulder of a hill, they found their way blocked by a small river in full flood. Standing on the bank was a young girl in a bright kimono, who was crying bitterly, for the water was too deep for her to attempt the crossing.

One of the monks, whom we shall call monk number one, went up to her and offered to carry her across the flood. Gladly she accepted and he took her up in his arms, carried her across and set her down on the further bank. Laughing happily and grateful she ran off and the two monks continued on their way. But now there was a change, for monk number two seemed to be preoccupied, depressed and monosyllabic. At last they got back to the monastery and separated for the night. After his devotions were over, monk number one fell asleep and slept the sleep of the just. Not so monk number two and soon there was a soft tap on the door and his anxious face looked into the cell. 'Brother, wake up! I am worried about your spiritual state', he whispered. 'You have sinned very grievously this afternoon. You know we are forbidden to look at a woman, what to say to touch her. Just think of your action. Go to the Abbot, Brother, and confess your sin. He will give you a penance and you may be saved.' 'Go to the Abbot yourself', said the sleepy voice of monk number one. 'I took that girl over the stream and set her down on the other side, but you are still carrying her.'

Monk number one had formed the habit of dictating to his mind, and his mind had formed the habit of obedience, so he was invulnerable, whilst the other monk was still at the mercy of both his mind and his emotions.

The other two essential items of discipline, the will and the imagination, should never stray apart from each other. Our Teacher has said that the will is a partial manifestation of the basic, central power of Consciousness. Therefore there is no such thing as a weak will, although there is a partial manifestation of that supreme will, which makes it appear vacillating and weak. This will, which is often so dimly manifested in us, is the power by which the passing products of the mind and the imagination are held steady for long enough for them to become actualities. When will and imagination are exercised separately, they are un-creative. Will divorced from imagination breeds blind obstinacy, a fixation, and the determination to carry through a performance come what may and whether it is good or bad. When the imagination is not supported by the will, the enervating habit of day-dreaming is born. The imagination gathers like clouds, produces mirage pictures which arouse desires, and then dissipates leaving a sense of frustration behind.

By imagination is not meant imaginings. For our purpose, imagination is the faculty which makes visual, or reveals, the quality of a percept or concept to the mind. It is like those fingers of light which used to creep across the dark sky during the barrage nights in the war. The blind will to meet a state of danger, or a situation unknown and unseen and yet known to be existing, was present. But that situation was made intelligible and manageable by those long beams of light. The pupil is often assailed by a barrage from an unknown quarter, and blind will and endurance will not save him, though will, if enlightened and directed by the beams of imagination, may do so.

Whether we are potential sages or get only a short way towards freedom in this incarnation, we shall have to make conscious use of these three items of spiritual

43

equipment: habit formation, imagination and will. Habits arise from a definite and conscious act, for when you decide to form a habit you also decide to prove your power of ascendancy over your mind. You are able to make this gesture by virtue of a partial recognition of your own true nature and perhaps also a blind or partial belief that all phenomena, of which your mind is a part, must necessarily be your instrument. This sense will deepen into certainty as the training proceeds. Habits are invested with life and power when regarded in this way.

If you decide to dictate to your mind, to embark on habit-forming, you must get to know your mind's capacity, as a man must get to know the engine of his car before he can drive it intelligently. There is a certain speed at which a car gives its best performance, and the same thing can be said about the mind. Blind intensity and acceleration will only destroy the mechanism in both cases, but one must always remember that what may be intense speed to me may be a dawdle to you, if you happen to be the owner of a Rolls-Royce car or a Rolls-Royce mind. The habit of moderation, which is a great asset in all undertakings, is that conscious process by which the performance is fitted to the capacity of an instrument, and it is a habit formed of judgement, control and also patience.

The will, when it works on its own, tends to be static and to produce tension. The imagination that functions by itself, as in chain-thinking and day-dreaming, and in the trivialities and moods produced in us as a sort of by-product, is also unprogressive and drains the vitality. Will and imagination work together in harmony and to perfection in a good meditation. The text is placed before the mind and it is held there for a certain time by the will exercised in relaxation, while it is savoured and made real through the exercise of imagination. As the meditation deepens, although both will and imagination are still present, it is only in a refined and subtle state.

To produce the decision to form a habit and then to bring the imagination into play, which sees the reason why it should be formed and visualises the results it may bring forth, means that you are making full use of your equipment. You should now be able to advance along the three paths at will, for it should always be remembered that this freedom, this capacity to become universal and not confined to one approach, is the traditional outcome of the Yoga training.

One of the Teachers in this line has said that there are some who collect facts as a squirrel collects nuts, but who have no devotion or reverence for knowledge itself, nor the impulse to pass it on where it is needed. Such a person is like a sackful of books animated by life. Then there is the man who is for ever active but who does not dedicate this activity to any higher power, and who never dreams of investigating the cause of his actions. This man is a danger to himself and to his fellow-men. Finally there is the devotee who puts nothing into practice but who worships blindly and impulsively, secure in his own atmosphere. This one is a joke to gods and men.

The teaching of Adhyatma Yoga is that the pupil's life must be a synthesis of all three paths. In the *World Within the Mind*, translated by Dr Shastri, it is said about the enlightened Yogi:

> The man of enlightened mind who is active in the world, and the illumined sage who sits in his

hermitage, are alike in their spiritual calm and have undoubtedly both reached the state of blessedness. Such a one is unconcerned whether he lives among the luxuries in his home, or retired from society and observing silence. It is all one to him. All is himself, and the whole universe without any partition or duality is within him - he is one with the supreme goal.

Now, at the last moment, the enquirer will probably wish to know whether there is some piece of equipment that he must discard in order that he may travel lighter. Oh yes, there is, but only one, for when that item has been discarded the traveller will receive wings, not limbs, with which to climb. This heavy piece of equipment is the ego, the little 'I'. It has been called the vehicle of duality, and it is the sole cause of fear. All Yoga practices are really devoted to its dethronement and to the installation of a new sovereign, the true 'I', which lies in secret glory behind the mind.

The traditional way by which the ego is unseated is through the practice of meditation. During his training, the pupil's time is divided between learning how best to order his daily life so that it provides a worthy preparation for meditation, and how to meditate when he arrives at that point.

V

DISCOVERY THROUGH ACTION

DISCOVERY through action plays a most important part in spiritual development. Action is one of the great teachers of Yoga, and until those discoveries have been made which only a right understanding of action can bring about, the final discovery which is made through deep meditation will only be made with difficulty, or perhaps it will never be made at all.

The way in which a pupil regards action, that is, whether he recoils from it or seeks it out, is an indication of the quality of his understanding of what he is being taught. His performance of action should improve as he progresses in knowledge. If this is not so, there is something wrong. Nearly every pupil at first looks on action as if it were a penance, or an intrusion. He fears that action might cause him to shift his attention from those spiritual things which he has assured himself can alone matter, back to the fascinations and activities of an active life. He is sure that such worldly things should not matter; nevertheless, they are still clamouring for attention at the back of his mind.

The training which Adhyatma Yoga offers consists of a process whereby an enquirer, having followed certain disciplines, succeeds in diverting his concentrated attention from the outer to the inner world. This makes it possible, in course of time, for a focus to be set up within him which will claim his love and service. After further instruction and meditation, such a focus, which can be an abstract concept or an inner visualisation, does arise within him, and he concentrates and meditates upon it. Later on, this focus loses its objective character and is recognised by the pupil as one with the Power residing within him, as his own Self - his centre. Finally, through the ultimate revelations of the philosophy, and his now intuitive understanding, he realises that this centre of Consciousness is not only within himself, but that it is the supreme reality or Truth - revealed to his awakened inner sense as all-pervading, the same within as without, and absolute.

Henceforth, whatever action he performs or whatever situation he finds himself in, he experiences no change in consciousness, for he is centred in this supreme and universal spirit - he is one with it. This transition from focused consciousness to being, is a transition which must be made by every serious follower of this Yoga, for it brings about the transition from dependence to freedom.

During this often lengthy process of spiritual unfoldment, action will serve as a sort of rain-gauge by which the weather prevailing in the pupil's mind can be discovered - whether it is dry or unsettled, stormy with attendant secondaries, or all clear. To speak in more sober terms, action reveals how far he is succeeding in transferring his preoccupation with outer activities to the inner, and, above all, what he understands to be the significance of this transference.

A pupil will pass through progressive stages with regard to action. At the beginning he is usually actuated by the ego-sense, by ambition or a desire for recognition and other palliatives. The actions he performs are therefore those which will further these individual ends. Later, through the instruction of his

Teacher and his own investigations, he awakens to the fact that he is not an isolated unit whose actions concern himself alone. He is a member of a universal family, and his actions have a universal as well as an individual significance. So now he sets to work to improve not only himself but the human family at large. This is usually known to him, it must be admitted, in the form of those around him; and in many cases his attentions are quite unnecessary and often very unwelcome.

This stage was tilted at by the old Chinese philosophers. It is said that one day a visitor went to see Lao Tzu and spoke to him about charity and duty to one's neighbour. Lao Tzu said: 'This talk of duty and charity drives me nearly crazy. Sir, by gentleness the hardest heart may be softened, but try to cut or polish it and it will glow like fire or freeze like ice. In the twinkling of an eye it will pass beyond the limit of the Four Seas. In repose perfectly still, in motion far away in the sky, no bolt can bar it, no bond can bind it - such is the human heart.'

Well, this may be so, but this stage is a necessary step in expansion and understanding, for through it a man's actions at least become ethical and benevolent. At last, but much later, as a result of training and purification through meditation, he becomes conscious of a Power greater than his own individual power. He succeeds in making this Power his focus and learns reverence and worship thereby. Now his actions slowly become selfless and dedicated, and for many this is the end of the spiritual journey.

But there is a higher purpose and a higher training than this, and it produces the means whereby the pupil, through direct inner perception, realises that the nature of this Power and of the Consciousness within him are one and the same. He knows that what he once worshipped as an objective focus has always been one with him, and yet universal. When he has arrived at this stage of knowledge, which is the highest state, his actions will fall into harmony with an unrevealed yet directed purpose, and they will have a universal significance.

The actions which take place in the empirical world have already been set in motion in the mental world. This fact forms the basis of the philosophy of action propounded in the *Bhagavad Gita*, the great scripture of India, and also in many of the classics of Vedanta. Although the people of the East are often classed as visionaries, there have been no thinkers who have realised more clearly the psychological importance of the nature of action. Ages ago they realised that if the fury of mental activity could be made to abate, physical action would inevitably fall into place. In the *Gita*, Shri Krishna, the Teacher of Prince Arjuna, tells his pupil that it is not by abstaining from action that he will win actionlessness. The man who sits with his physical organs of action perfectly restrained, isolated and apparently actionless, but who is all the time thinking in his mind on the objects of action, is said to be self-deluded. It is only he who can control his senses by his mind and then direct his organs of action how to act, who is the adept and who excels.

When the pupil takes up this training, he must perforce accept many axioms which he cannot as yet prove, just as a student of chemistry must accept the statements of the teacher as to the ingredients and quantities needed to make a successful experiment. In the same way, the pupil's grasp of the supreme truth of non-duality must necessarily be theoretical for a long time. There are very few of us who have not deluded ourselves on this point, through ignorance of how long it takes before theoretical knowledge turns into direct and positive conviction. The best way of gauging how far what one professes to believe has entered the blood stream, or rather into the mind stream, is to watch one's reactions. In other words, it is to study those acts which take place before memory and reason have had time to step in and smooth things over. These reactions will immediately reveal the hidden source which provides their motive power. The acid test of conviction can only be made through action and reaction, and this holds good till the moment of liberation comes.

The tendency of an untrained man to identify himself with his activities, bodily and mental, shows that he is under the impression that reality is to be found in them. Reality spells security, and security postulates the end of a search. A man may tell himself that he is an eternal hunter who enjoys the chase for the sake of the chase alone. But this is not so. He only hunts because he tacitly assumes that one day he will catch up with his quarry and rest in the enjoyment of its possession.

This capacity for identification, whether with outer objects or inner concepts such as grief, joy, action or inaction, is a manifestation of a fundamental characteristic in man - a quality which will in the end lead him out of his prison. One of the principal lessons he has to learn during his training is when to use his capacity for identification and when to withhold it - not *how* to identify himself, that is too easy, but what to identify himself with.

Whatever the mind identifies itself with, to that it

gives reality. This is because the consciousness it brings to bear on the concept holds the nature of reality within itself. Identification with any object, whether tangible or intangible, precludes the possibility of regarding that object objectively - that is, it destroys the sense of separateness and independence in the observer. Therefore, in order to recognise the component parts and qualities of an object, a certain distance has to be maintained, to enable the investigation to be carried out in focus. Identification, on the other hand, involves a merging with the object and a consequent submerging of the independent judgement.

When the final spiritual identification takes place, we are told that there is a final merging of the subject-object relationship and a submerging of the independent personal sense and judgement, through identification and unity with the supreme Reality. It is the deep, yet hidden knowledge of this which lies at the root of man's impulse to unite and identify himself with objects and concepts.

If this is so, the next discovery which the pupil must make is how to disidentify himself from his actions - how to look upon himself as a director of action and not as a doer of action. As described in the *Gita*, he must first learn to control his senses by his mind. It is only after this control has been achieved that his organs of action are directed to the work. A director of a factory does not sweat in tense anxiety, that is, if he is a good director, with a good work force under him. He gives his orders and sees that they are carried out. It is not for him to identify himself with the actual work, only with the motive for the work and its due carrying out. In the same way, action should first be conceived consciously by the mind and then carried out as a reaction by the organs of action. This mental control and the spontaneous response by the organs of action becomes automatic in time.

Our Teacher used to say in another connection: 'What would you think of a man who studied every word in a sentence separately, its derivation and its individual meaning, but failed to apply himself to finding out the meaning of the whole sentence?' In our rawness we used to think to ourselves: 'Can there really be such people? Surely not!' But this is just what some of us, and a great many men and women who are not in training, do in relation to action. A word in a sentence has two facets - its specific meaning, and its significance in the sentence, and so it is with action. Following this analogy, the immediate and particular meaning of any single action is the immediate reason for its performance. 'I must do this because ...' or 'I dislike doing this, but it's my duty. I'll do it, but as a penance.' 'I'm doing it because I like to.' But when its purpose and wider meaning is considered, each action will be seen to possess a wider significance, like the word in the sentence. Tangled up as we are in the performance of isolated action, we are like children stumbling over the pronunciation of single words in a foreign tongue. We flounder on, till not even the immortal gods could make sense of the reason or the outcome of our activities.

In order to recognise the purpose and inner character of a thing, we have said that a certain distance must be kept between the observer and the thing under observation. This is the reason why the practice of dispassion and disidentification is advocated so strongly in all spiritual schools. 'Yoga', says the *Gita*, 'is skill in living.' You may be sure this includes skill in action, and throughout the *Gita* are found instructions as to how the learner may obtain this skill.

The method and progression have already been outlined, but this is so important and so often misunderstood that it bears repetition. Through meditation and conscious control, which means through conscious direction of the mental force, the pupil slowly purifies his perceptions and his inner atmosphere. This makes it possible for him to recognise within himself the presence of a Power, which manifests intermittently at first, but which later reveals itself as the ever-present all-pervasive reality, or God.

This discovery takes place as the result of inner, not outer action - inner action in the form of deep meditation. When the disciple grows aware of the transformation it has brought about, a compelling impulse awakens in him to worship this supreme Truth, or God, with a love one-pointed and intense. In the words of the great Ramanuja Acharya, this love 'asks nothing but the honour and delight of serving Him'.

In order to be served with a love one-pointed and intense, this supreme Power, or spirit, abstract by nature, will have to be invested with attributes, so that it may become the focus before which all action may be laid as an offering. Shri Krishna, the Teacher in the *Bhagavad Gita*, an Avatar or direct descent of this spirit into matter, says to his pupil Prince Arjuna:

> The world is action-bound except where action is performed as an offering to the Lord. Therefore, O Arjuna, perform action as a sacrifice only, and be devoid of attachment. Whatever you do, whatever you eat, whatever you give away (in other words, whatever action you perform), let it be carried out

as an offering to Me. Then, with mind controlled, centred on the Self, ridding yourself of hope and fear, fight - your fever gone.

Here Shri Krishna mentions the Self, or the supreme and abstract Power, and also Himself, who is that Power when embodied as the divine focus. It is the same Self, but presented in the world of phenomena as an object for man's worship. Shri Krishna was such an Avatar, as was the Lord Jesus, appearing for the objective worship and enlightenment of men throughout the ages.

Now this is the secret method or discipline by which the chain of egoity which binds man so tightly and which makes him identify himself with his acts, may be loosened. For it is through this means that action, whatever its immediate cause, is invested with a purpose more far-reaching than its surface one. In the Sufi classic, the *Masnavi* of Rumi, it says: 'The action which is born of your mind and your emotions, clings to your skirts like your own child.' Such action doesn't want to grow up. The practice of offering all action to the supreme spirit, to God, will enable the action to grow in stature and so trouble you no longer.

There is a poem by Nirbhaya Rama which describes this discipline of looking upon all action as an opportunity for service. Here are some of the verses:

> In whatever you do with your hands, avoid
>   harming any living being.
> This is called 'Service of the great God,
>   whose glory none can declare'.
> As you advance, leave behind all thought
>   of gain or loss.

This is called 'Circumambulation of the great
   Lord' - know it well.
Look with reverence on all that is an object
   of the mind or senses;
Know phenomenal existence to be the body
   of the Lord and His abode.
Harbour love for all beings and lay aside
   all sense of difference.
This is called 'Devotion to God'.
He is in all, yet He transcends all;
His nature is existence, consciousness
   and bliss.
This is an undoubted fact.
Make your intellect space-like, negating all
   name and form.
This is called 'Adoration of God, who is
   taintless and all-pervasive'.
Establish yourself in the Witness Consciousness,
   disregard all day-dreams;
This is called 'The highest meditation on
   the august Lord'.
Says Nirbhaya Rama: Worship God in this way,
   and you need follow no other discipline.
This is the way to perfect illumination.

This is one way and an exalted way, yet there is
another and it has already been described, but must be
outlined again at this point. The teaching states that
reality, or Truth, is omniscient. It is, as Consciousness, the substratum of all phenomena, that is, of all
gross as well as subtle matter. If this is so, the pupil
must, and will, win a direct knowledge of this through
the final meditations. When he sees this Truth directly,
he will cease to be able to make a cleavage between

matter and spirit. He will become universally based, and secure in the knowledge that the supreme Truth is all, and he is That.

The one who chooses this last way, will pursue it to its only conclusion. Through identification with the supreme Light, he will become his own light and a light to others. Thus he will reach freedom. Now, as Chuang Tzu says, he employs his mind as a mirror. A mirror grasps nothing, it refuses nothing. It receives but it does not keep. Acting thus, he triumphs over matter without injury to himself, and surely with great spiritual benefit to all mankind. This final discovery is thus made by the actualisation, through inspired action, of this truth of non-duality.

This is the state of consciousness in which the illumined seers and sages live their lives and perform action. True spirituality is always accompanied by a manifestation of intense spiritual energy and vitality. There are hundreds of examples taken from all religions in support of this: the Lord Buddha, St Teresa of Avila, Shri Shankaracharya and, in our own times, Shri Dadaji of Aligarh - the Teacher of our Teacher - our Teacher himself and, taken from another spiritual stream, that great Jewish light, Leo Baeck. Although Leo Baeck was not an acknowledged Yogi, these last three were in the highest tradition of Adhyatma Yoga, for they lived in both worlds simultaneously and worked indiscriminately in both.

Action, therefore, provides an outward and visible indication of the presence or absence of spiritual understanding. The so-called discoveries which are made through it are in fact confirmations, by practical tests, of the findings made intuitively by a disciple while engaged in the progressive and inner activity of meditation. As the speculations of the pupil are turned into certainties, he acquires a sense of freedom and mastery, which reveals itself in his detached and relaxed action.

At the last stage, as has been said, the pupils go forward on two different paths in order to reach the same objective. The devotee takes the path of devotion, of contemplation and service of the God with attributes, or an Avatar, or a saint. In the course of time, that focus will reveal itself to him as the supreme reality, and thus he will attain freedom. The goal of the second type of disciple is reached through the path of knowledge, by which at last he too reaches the state where the fact of the supreme reality or Truth is confirmed within him, and is revealed as one with his own Self, which he now knows to be omnipresent and one-without-a-second.

Perhaps such a training may sound alarming and impossible to attempt, but when our Teacher painted it to us in words, and by his living example showed the harmonious and free state of one who had reached its goal, his pupils felt that it must be possible for all! And so it is, provided that the pupil is willing to pay the price, which is application, devotion, obedience, and above all patience to await results. The length of time he can give to the practices is the least important item in his training; the first essential is that he shall bring his imagination and intelligence to bear on his efforts.

VI

THE MAN OF ENLIGHTENED ACTION

IT IS DIFFICULT to say why, but there appears to be a lurking feeling in many people's minds that a practical and active life is less spiritual than an intellectual one, and again, that an intellectual life is less spiritual than a contemplative one. They apparently think that only those who cannot make a success of the inner life should be asked to serve in a practical capacity, and give a practical demonstration of spiritual principles, and that the necessity for action diminishes as a man rises, until at last it ceases altogether and he can retire from the life of the world, if he so desires.

This of course can and does happen in some cases but it is not the rule; indeed nothing could be less fundamentally true than the assumption from which it springs. In Adhyatma Yoga, withdrawal from the world is not advocated, and only those who have served a long apprenticeship of practical service are allowed to become monks and contemplatives. Our Teacher, Dr Shastri, was definite about this point; he even dignified the distortion of the philosophy from which the idea of retirement springs, with the name of 'heresy'. According to him, in order to hold this view, a fundamental cleavage must have been made between matter and spirit. The philosophy of Advaita Vedanta recognises no such thing, matter and spirit being held to be one in essence though seemingly separate in manifestation. He used to say that India, which is the home of the doctrine of non-duality, had suffered grievously and would continue to suffer, for having countenanced this heresy, through the adoption of untouchability and its offshoots.

In the West we are not consistent, for although we may appear to believe in the higher value of a life devoted to contemplation, when it comes to a practical working out of this theory, we throw it over. We choose instead the priest who is also a good footballer - a muscular Christian, he used to be called - for we think that he will have more weight with his parishioners than one who is more at home in the high atmosphere of the spirit. We still appear to work on the assumption that men are more attracted by what they can understand and are used to, than by that which they desire to understand.

The teaching of the Vedanta is that the spirit is pure, non-dual, all-pervasive and fundamental. Matter only exists, or rather appears to exist, by virtue of the reality and existence of spirit, on which it is based and on which it depends. If this were not so, chaos would be the only certainty in life, and the truth of Advaita would be disproved.

It has been said somewhere that if this Truth - the truth of Advaita - is a fact, then nothing else matters, but if it is false, nothing matters at all, and this is so. But we have the words and also the example of certain men who have no interest in spreading opinions, only in revealing the Truth. They have seen this Truth more clearly than we see the physical appearance of matter. Their testimony is that through training and self-purification, reality, or God, can be directly seen. It is then that man experiences the non-dual Truth directly and knows himself to be one with it. Direct experience alone convinces and it is direct experience which is the acknowledged goal of the disciple. Until he reaches it, he must watch and follow those who have attained it, for they are liberal-hearted men who will impart the Truth to the one who really seeks to know, when he is ready to receive it.

Our Teacher has said that this direct recognition of Truth and the passing on of it to others, is the normal process in spiritual development. In a biological sense an organism is not complete until it has reproduced itself, and this is true in an inner sense of the yogi. From time to time men are born or are produced by spiritual training who, by their revealed outer life and their inner strength and compassion, show the way to liberation to both devotees and sinners.

The holy Teacher and sage Shri Shankaracharya was such a doer of enlightened action; from him onwards - and before him, no doubt - the practical demonstration of directly cognised Truth, through constructive action, has been held to be the natural and desirable outcome of spiritual realisation. When this stage is reached, action is not sought, and only those actions which come of their own accord, so to say, are intuitively performed. Such a man has freed himself from all prejudices and, what is much more important, from all preferences. St Francis kissed the lips of the leper at an early stage in his career, but it took a lifetime of training and illumined vision to enable him to open his hands and allow the keys and the policy of his beloved Order to fall into the grasp of another.

In our own times, a very great karma yogi indeed and one who was also a great teacher, an inspiration to those in bondage and agony, was the Rabbi Leo Baeck. He seems to have been completely at home in both the world of material things and the spiritual world. So natural and perfect was his understanding and manipulation of both these worlds that no-one who appreciates his spiritual eminence would dream of limiting him to either category. As our revered Teacher would have said: 'He was a hundred per cent man', and that praise coming from him always implied that the man was amphibious - at home in both elements.

There is no need to go into the details of his life in peace and war, except to say that he was arrested and released again several times by the Germans, until in 1943 he was at last sent to the concentration camp for Jews at Theresienstadt, from which few emerged except to go to the gas chamber. There he lived and worked until the end of the war and beyond that. His spirit was so resilient, so at home in every situation and condition, that he seems to have dwelt in this camp as he would have lived and worked in a spiritual community. If one has to summarise the contribution he made to those around him, and to those also whom he never met, but who have come to hear of his pure mind and unbreakable spirit, it would be that he lived out practically the yogic dictum: 'Inner growth, not endurance'. When such a pronouncement is interpreted by one who is based and interpenetrated by spirit, it means constant expansion towards the Light, and no acceptance of the darkness of ignorance and duality.

He was a leader, a teacher, a scholar and one of the spiritually great. His understanding of the inner life and its potentialities was the outcome of his recognition of the universal power of God and the brotherhood of man - what the yogis would call the universality of consciousness. Through the play of destiny, the Nazi guard who had so terribly maltreated and tortured this group of prisoners in the beginning, became prisoners to them in turn. When this happened, not only did the Rabbi Baeck turn aside the natural desire for revenge in his fellow Jews, but in the end, no prisoner in that camp harboured that desire. This was due to his example, or perhaps to the fact that though the possibility of revenge must have entered his mind in connection with those under his care, it never rested there for an instant. He taught all in that prison to look upon their plight as a challenge to their faith and ingenuity, and as an opportunity for interior growth. This involved a determination on his part to promote knowledge of all kinds amongst them and at all times. It is said that when he gave his philosophical discourses in that camp after lights were out, seven hundred listeners hung on his words like clusters of grapes.

Our Teacher has always said, and Rabbi Leo Baeck lived this belief, that the man who ceases to learn or to desire to learn, ceases to live as a human being. If a man, having received knowledge, has no desire to share it when it is sought, he holds up the natural and healthy process of circulation in the collective mental body. It is indeed a spiritual rule that what has been received must be passed on in some form or other, at the proper time, and that to disregard this law is sin. The exchange may be by word of mouth or from mind to mind, or its transference may remain hidden - a movement in the upper air of the spirit - but it must take place when the necessity arises. This is why the giving away in charity of a part of the material possessions of a pupil is advocated in all the spiritual schools; it is a practical living out of this spiritual ideal.

The Rabbi Leo Baeck himself once wrote: 'The spiritual does not merely hover overhead like a pure conception; it consists in the being and quality of the individuals who have won it for their own.' This ideal of activity on both planes is not new. It has been cherished in the East and West throughout the ages, though often misunderstood and stifled by the world as unfitting. The belief which makes this ideal natural and inevitable has no special home in any one religion and even the ways in which it is practically demonstrated differ. In the Vedanta, the vision is of a universal Consciousness, which is the basis of every manifestation. While the outer eye still sees variety and good and evil, it lies unrevealed, but when the inner eye is opened, Consciousness is found to be that which pervades all and is fundamental in all, like the *akasha* or space. Then the knower moves about, blown by the wind of the spirit, giving help, encouragement or enlightenment as he is prompted to do.

In Christianity this knowledge is expressed as the belief in the all-present God, manifest in his recognisable form as Jesus Christ, who makes all men active and one in his service. The love of God is based on wisdom and can be expressed in action, but direct knowledge of God is revealed through the essence of the being of the illumined sage alone. Then, as has been said, he may act, but it is his spiritual effulgence which enlightens.

All beliefs are theoretical and they represent only a section of the whole Truth. But when the Truth, which is beyond words or description, breaks in its fullness upon the inner sense, the inner and outer intention fuse into one. The man sees the miracle of perfection and not merely the reason for it, and he becomes free. When this takes place, his very presence in the world enriches and feeds it, though his true status may be unrecognised, and when he acts, nothing can withstand him.

The sun in its original, pristine state is a glorious yet an awful thing. No-one could approach it and live. But all that we experience of its marvels is that it looks like a round ball of light which seems to rise and set, that it is the home of light, that it gives us food and warmth and fills our hearts and bodies with strength and joy. The enlightened man is just such an awful yet glorious being. We could not approach him if the light which he now is were directly revealed. Therefore, all we know of him is that he dispenses gifts of various kinds and appears to accept them; that he gives us his companionship and withdraws it; and that he brings on our growth by his visible presence and his invisible power - in fact that he lives among us as one of ourselves.

Our Teacher used to tell us that the object of growth was to transcend, not to enhance, existing circum-stances. Transcendence is the culmination of growth - the spiritually adult state. At present this state is known to us through the indirect testimony of those who have attained it. It is only directly recognisable by those who are approaching, or have reached that state themselves.

The lives of the great - not only the supremely great, but the lesser luminaries also - are manifestations of selfless, constructive action. These men are the embodiments of encouragement. They demonstrate for us that the spiritual ideals work, by living them before us. They invest every occasion and happening with spiritual significance, and if you can say such a thing, they ruthlessly and consciously turn every situation to spiritual advantage. As this advantage is to everyone's advantage, it is not such an egoistic performance as it sounds.

There are those who hold that if you try to live a spiritual life or belong to a spiritual community, you immediately become the target for tests, trials and adverse happenings, and that if your progress is uneventful, it is no progress at all. But anyone who has even a superficial knowledge of the horrors and tragedies which can and do happen to those who live in the world, will admit that a large proportion of the human race are daily passing through worse trials than can be imagined by a sheltered mind. These trials are faced without any guidance of a spiritual nature at all. The yogi or the spiritual aspirant is only sharing the common lot of man and should be in a far better position to bear it than his brothers in the world. For he has received the knowledge and training which should enable him to regard every event as a challenge and an opportunity for growth.

This is perhaps one of the greatest contributions made by Rabbi Leo Baeck. He did not, if I understand him aright, try to steer his boat of suffering souls away from the dark shore and to land them on the other shore - the shore of light. For him there was no other shore, there was no need to move at all, or to make a dangerous journey. He believed that spiritual truth and safety lay directly beneath their feet and that they had only to uncover it there, to see it and rest in it. In his sonnet 'On Homer's Blindness', Keats says:

Aye, on the shores of darkness there is light,
The precipices show untrodden green;
There is a budding morrow in midnight;
There is a triple sight in blindness keen.

So Leo Baeck believed and so he taught by his example, and so do all the spiritually great. No need to travel to find the security of Truth, it is there, near at hand, and waiting to be revealed. So it was with our most revered Teacher. No need to manufacture an atmosphere, to have a set of symbols or special conditions through which alone the truth of the spirit would become knowable. That Truth could be revealed, and it was revealed and passed on to his pupils, according to each one's capacity, anywhere and at any time. He only admitted the necessity of probing deeper and deeper beneath the appearance of an ordinary happening in order to uncover it.

He used to tell the story of a Teacher who suddenly told two of his pupils to dig for water in a most unlikely piece of ground. They started with enthusiasm, but when they had gone down some feet and found nothing, they stopped and returned to the Teacher and told him there was no water in the place he had selected. 'Dig deeper', was all he said; so back they went. After they had gone down a few more feet, they gave up once again and went back to the Teacher to try to persuade him to give up the idea once and for all. But he still said: 'Dig deeper, my sons'. Back they went and worked for some time, and then one of them said: 'I'm going to stop - there's no water here'. The other went on doggedly, and suddenly the water was there before his eyes.

So it is in the spiritual sense. The depth at which water will be found differs, but there is not an inch of earth under which it does not lie, and the spiritual drills can go very deep! This knowledge is as a beacon of hope, and it helps the aspirant on.

At this stage, belief in the existence of reality, or

God, must still remain theoretical, but none the less to have such a belief at all is a very great possession indeed. Later, when the spirit is directly revealed and recognised in every place, and for all time, it will cease to be a possession or a belief. It will be revealed to the one who knows it as his own nature.

These may seem to be mere words, for they refer to things which perhaps cannot be expressed in words, but the Truth which they are trying to describe is the heritage of each one of us. Such descriptions, however inadequate, are attempts to augment our longing for that Truth and for the expansion and freedom it brings. It is also essential to understand why we should make sacrifices, why we should voluntarily restrict ourselves, however temporarily, and above all, why we should attempt to undergo a spiritual training and discipline at all. If we keep our eyes on the men of illumined action, we shall learn the answers to these questions from them and from their example, and they will give us strength to press on.

What, then, is the ordinary man to do if he wishes to locate and bring to the fore the powers which lie at the back of his mortal mind and senses, and which will reveal his immortality to him? He must first intensify his desire to emerge from his present state of slavery to his mind and from the fear that goes with it. Secondly, he must himself approach the Truth, and not rely solely on those who know about it, or on merely reading about it. He must strive to approach it through his own stretching out - that is, by simple meditation and spiritual practices such as the repetition of a name of God with imagination and faith, or a virtue such as courage, patience or compassion, and also through exercises in visualisation. In this way he will change his sense of values and will become as harmless as a snake that has had its fangs removed. This is a prerequisite for the spiritual aspirant, although he will still be able to hiss a little when necessary, which is another desirable characteristic. He must widen his sphere of sympathy also, through enquiry and reading, and so break down the adhesions of likes and dislikes, superiority and inferiority. Thus he will become more open to instruction and to the influence of the great spiritual powers - for conscious effort evokes a response.

According to the code of the sea, signals for help must always be answered. Even a little sailing boat can stop a great battleship in its course if it sends out signals of distress. The spiritual practices may be regarded as signals for help and guidance, and they will inevitably attract a response if they are made - and from great and powerful vessels too!

To make efforts consciously and with imagination and determination is to obey the law we mentioned in connection with the Rabbi Leo Baeck: 'Inner growth, not endurance'.

VII

ACTION AND BEYOND

ACTION is that which influences our future, perhaps one should say 'the future', and therefore it is most important for us to understand it correctly. Action is not confined to the outer organ - the body - but also includes the activity of the inner organ - the *antahkarana*. The highest authority on action is the *Bhagavad Gita*, and there is no book in which the psychology of action has been examined so subtly and exhaustively.

Action in itself is not decried in the *Gita* or in any other classic of Adhyatma Yoga. It is only when action is used by man as a vehicle for his personal desires - the release of his *vasanas*, or latent tendencies - that the warning is given. Prince Arjuna, in the *Gita*, far from being told not to act, is told that he must act, and is instructed how to act. It is not action that hinders, but the idea that you are doing it. As long as you identify yourself with an action and its results, you weaken yourself by laying yourself open to the inheritance of the ramification of events the action brings in its train. This sense of identity also goes directly contrary to the central teaching of Advaita: non-identification.

There is a story in the *Vishnu Purana* which describes how once in the remote ages the *devas* and the *asuras* (the forces of light and darkness) met in a great pitched battle. All the *asuras* were eventually killed and nothing but *devas* remained. They lived peaceful lives of contemplation for a long time, and there was no shadow of discord anywhere. Then the Lord stirred and became aware of - what? The satisfactory nature of His creation? No! He became aware of a want of variety, a monotony, a want of richness, and He enquired into the matter. As a result He created thousands of new *asuras*, and soon the sway and variety of *sansara*, the world process, was resumed and the Lord professed Himself satisfied.

Another story tells of the seven mind-born sons of Brahma who, when they were introduced into *sansara*, refused to take any part in the drama, but sat in contemplation, begetting neither sons nor works. Here again the Lord pronounced Himself dissatisfied and He created the great sages, Vasishtha and many others, who took wives and lived lives of cosmic and earthly value.

The moral of these stories is that action, far from being considered deplorable and to be avoided, is held to be the very essence of *sansara*, which, after all, is of divine origin. Action must not only continue if the world is to continue, but the Lord has decreed that it *shall* continue. Each of these points is made in clear language in the first few chapters of the *Gita*.

Now if, as is shown here, action as action is countenanced in the philosophy, where does the difficulty arise? The difficulty lies in understanding what is the right way to act and to look on action.

The Chinese, who thoroughly understand the laws governing right action, say that if a man playing a game plays only for a counter, he will play well. If he stakes his girdle (which is a precious possession in China) he will be nervous, and if he plays for yellow gold, he will lose his wits. His skill is the same in each case, but he is distracted by the value of the stakes. This shows that

71

everyone who attaches importance to the external (the fruits) becomes internally without resources.

According to the *Gita*, action itself cannot lead to God. It leads to *karma* (the chain of cause and effect) and the upholding of *sansara*, and *karma* leads to endless future births and deaths. Yoga may be said to be nothing other than the completion or liquidating of *karma*. It is the science of purified and enlightened action, as a result of which knowledge is unveiled and *karma* is arrested and finally brought to a standstill. Action does not lead to God, but the offering of action and its fruits to Him, does. Therefore the right and traditional way to act is to act in such a manner that the actions do not bind - to perform action as an agent or an actor, without any sense of responsibility or doership. Actions when performed in this way have results, it is true, but these results do not involve the man who performs them. They fulfil a cosmic and not an individual purpose.

Directly it is said that man should undertake action as an actor or agent, and not as an instigator, many people jump to the conclusion that an irresponsible, *laissez-faire*, drawling attitude to life is recommended. But when we go to a play, we do not expect to see an actor slouch across the stage and say in an aside to the audience: 'Don't blame me, I didn't write the play.' No, we expect to see him play with as much intensity as if he were living the part, perhaps with more, and so does the great audience of the almighty gods expect us to act our parts in the cosmic drama, as they are written, without adding or leaving out a single word.

The sense of being an inaugurator of an act is bound up with success and faiiure. It must be so, and it is idle to tell anyone to inaugurate or undertake works and at the same time not to care for the result. This feat might be accomplished ninety-nine times out of a hundred, but the failure on the hundredth will expose the whole false reasoning. The only way to perform works so that not only do they not bind man, but actively further his progress, is to perform them as a sacrifice to the Lord, looking on oneself as His devotee.

At this point people will say to themselves: 'Yes, but not every kind of action can be performed in this way. There is more than one kind of action. What is the answer to that?'

Dr Shastri has explained that action may be considered under three main categories:

1. Automatic, instinctive action or reaction.
2. Self-conscious or desire-directed action.
3. Supra-conscious or cosmically directed action.

The unconscious, instinctive class of action is the common reaction of all phenomena - including man - to stimuli, such as the opening of the bud to the warmth and light of the sun, the purring of the kitten by the fire, the smack of the hand on the mosquito, digestion and so forth.

In the second category, the desire-directed actions are undertaken to gratify that central point of consciousness in man which he calls his self. The problem of right action and its working out is confined to this class. Actions which take place in the first class are too rudimentary, and in the third too impersonal and high, for feelings of egoity to intrude. It is the belief of man that he is the instigator of action that constitutes the danger in action. Therefore the ego-directed, desire-formulated class of action is the only class we need to consider. It is the duty of man to learn to control his action in this category and finally to transcend it and to act only according to the laws of the third category. When he has learnt to do this, he is said to be a servant or instrument of God, and the cosmic purpose can be furthered through him.

Now a word about the process called perception, which precedes and is the cause of every action. Speaking generally, the yogic teaching is that man has three bodies - the causal, the subtle and the physical. These bodies correspond to the three stages of perception. The causal body is the cosmic knower, the container within itself of all phenomena in a seed form. It does not look outward, it looks inward upon itself and what it reflects. The subtle body is the inner organ - the *antahkarana* - which perceives this causal seed as phenomena, as it appears in the subtle plane, looks outward at it, classifies it and selects and reacts to it. The physical or outer organ - arms, ears, tongue and so forth - carries out on the physical plane the reactions instigated by the subtle body or *antahkarana*.

Each of the three organs or bodies operates on a different plane of consciousness and perceives the so-called objects as they manifest on that plane. Thus the causal consciousness, operating on the causal plane, sees objects in their seed or causal form. The subtle organ or *antahkarana*, operating on the subtle plane, sees objects in their subtle form. This makes it easier to understand what the philosophers of Vedanta mean when they say that the forces of the *antahkarana* go outward and take the shape of the object observed. The word 'shape' in this context does not refer to the physical shape but to the subtler aspect of the object, its essence, or the 'shape' of its qualities. When this has been assessed by the *antahkarana*, it is passed on to the outer organ. The object is then seen in terms of the physical medium - shapes, bodies, masses of matter, formulated ideas and so forth.

The movement of unhindered force is outward from subtle to gross. The movement of controlled force is a return from the gross to the causal. This is the path of Yoga and this is the way in which the circle of unfoldment is completed.

Having traced very superficially how perception takes place, we must try and find out what gives the objects of perception the capacity to awaken desire in man and so to stimulate him to action. According to the logic of an ordinary uninstructed person, the acquisition of practically any object, physical or subtle, must produce power, and give increased liberty or freedom. Therefore the possibility of amassing material wealth or subtle power or knowlege, causes a picture of the state where these things become his to arise in the *antahkarana* of the man, through the exercise of the picture-building, planning, castle-in-the-air faculty known as *sankalpa*. He then makes the gestures, or puts into motion those causes which will produce the effects he desires. Effects are produced in this way, but the interesting point is that they do not produce the increased power and freedom which the man envisaged. Whether the outcome of a specific act be considered good or bad, it will certainly produce an occasion or cause for a further action. The man, far from enjoying greater liberty, is more closely bound than ever.

This applies to the man in the process of self-discovery. After countless disappointments, he stands knowingly or unknowingly at the beginning of a path of self-training. He comes to the conclusion that he must not snatch at each and every thing, but must select - select what he considers good for himself, and not only for himself but for others. It is this stage that Chuang Tzu describes when he says that the well-intentioned start 'tripping up people over charity and fettering them with duty to their neighbours'. Then he says: 'What with their gushing over music and fussing over ceremony, the empire becomes divided against itself.' In other words, man becomes confused and divided against himself.

We have shown that a man performs and will always be obliged to perform, certain instinctive acts, but that through education he starts to learn how to select and confine these acts to the class to which they belong. He learns to select still further in the second category and engages in those actions which he thinks are going to benefit himself and, at a slightly more enlightened stage, which are going to benefit others. At this point he does a good deal of interfering harm. How is he going to pass from the fussy, grandmotherly, responsible, busy state to the state of divine recklessness of the ideal man of the *Gita* - the man of repose, absorption, and yet of instant perception and reaction? The great Ramanuja Acharya says: 'The cardinal doctrine of the *Gita* is love of God, one-pointed and intense, which asks nothing but the honour and the delight of serving Him.'

This state of consciousness comes as the direct result of the purificatory discipline of the Yoga. When the pupil begins to envisage it in his inner life, he automatically starts making the necessary changes in his active life. Then, as the invisible vision of the Supreme takes up more and more of his time, his mind and his heart, he finds that he is performing those actions

which come before him, automatically, and offering
their fruits, good and bad, to God, while concentrating
his heart in devotion and preoccupation on Him. The
time will come when he will be incapable of saying any
more: 'This is an action and I am doing it for a
particular reason'. He will have become so preoccupied
that he will move like a dancer following music. He
will have ceased to wonder why he is doing this or that
particular action, for he will realise that he can never
know.

Don't say: 'It can't be done'. If it is impossible,
the higher teachings of Yoga are not possible and the
whole structure falls to the ground.

Those who still obstinately hanker to give, to serve,
to place their gifts and powers at the feet of, are all
clinging to the beginning of class two. They have really
only one duty - one action - which they must perform
and that is to carry out the practices given to them. If
they do so, the day will come when they will realise
that they have nothing to give because they are nothing
- not 'less-than-the-dust' nothing, but nothing
individual and separate. They are not separate entities.
They are That which they have been contemplating,
and His purposes are their purposes, His strength is
their strength - they are one.

This, of course, is the goal and the summit, but
before that, the one who has that goal strongly before
his eyes thinks of many plays, tricks and practices to
make it come quickly. Shri Shankara in his poem on
'Mental Worship' says:

> Thou art my *Atman*; my intellect is thy consort;
> my sense organs are thy attendants; this body is thy
> temple; ministering to the senses is my worship of

thee; my sleep is *samadhi*; my moving about on
foot is the act of circumambulation; all the words I
speak are hymns to thee; whatever works I do are
thy worship, O Lord. Glory be to thee.

Everything should be pressed into the service so that the
mind shall never forget its purpose for one minute and
the *vritti* (mental modification, or 'wave in the sea of
the mind') *Kham Brahman* - All is God - may be
established. This is the only way to transcend
separative action: purify the *antahkarana* so that
perceptions do not lodge in the *manas*, the lower mind,
but pass directly to *buddhi*, the higher intellect, which
dwells at the confluence of *jiva* and *Atman* (the
individual self and the universal Self).

The last six chapters of the *Gita* are full of
descriptions of the enlightened being - the man of
cosmic action, who does not perform actions but
through whom actions are performed, and you can read
them and should do so very often. Chuang Tzu has
given us a description of such a person:

The repose of the sage is not what the world calls
repose. His repose is the result of his mental
attitude. All creation could not disturb his
equilibrium - hence his repose. To be in accord
with man is human happiness. To be in accord with
God is the happiness of God. Thus in ancient
times, Shun asked the Chinese Emperor Yao:
'How does your Majesty employ his faculties?'
'I am not arrogant towards the defenceless; I do
not neglect the poor; I grieve for those who die; I
succour the orphan; I sympathise with the widow.
Beyond that - nothing.'

'Good indeed', cried Shun, 'but not yet great.'
'How so?' enquired Yao.
'Be passive', said Shun, 'like the virtue of God.'
(The meaning is: 'Be above the pairs of opposites - impartial.') 'The sun and the moon shine, the seasons revolve, day and night alternate, the clouds come and the rain falls.' (In other words, the cosmic play goes on.)
'Alas', cried Yao, 'what a muddle I have been making! You are in accord with God, whereas I have been in accord with the standards of men.'

VIII

EXPANSION

IN THE VEDANTA philosophy the word 'expansion' means the approach to that state which bestows joy, security and fearlessness on a man, which is another way of saying that it is the outer sign of an increasing awareness of the supreme Consciousness or God. The process of expanding the mind takes the form of giving it, through the training of mind control, the ability to concentrate on a single point, and the fruit of this will be the power to expand to infinity in meditation.

The seeds of expansion are in all things, manifesting as a sense of growth and direction and the urge for fulfilment. Man's excursions into the different spheres of activity - emotional, intellectual and mystical - are made inevitable by this urgency to expand. For when it comes to man's secret business with himself - to what he fundamentally desires - this turns out to be that he may break away from the subservient state in which he has been ordered to do this or be that by the ego, and come to rest in some positive and free state, which we know to be the state of a knower of God.

Man's conception of freedom changes as he grows in awareness, but all along he is faintly conscious of its existence and of his desire to experience its power. Imprisonment is shunned by all. It is the punishment meted out by man to his fellow men when they transgress the accepted code of laws, and it is the punishment which the mind itself metes out to man when he transgresses the inner code of laws and maltreats his mind by denying it the right to grow and expand.

This mind, or centre of reacting awareness, is in fact the only object in man to be investigated and trained. It is composed of various levels of awareness, presided over by the ego-sense and, in a more hidden and subtle way, by a ray of divine Consciousness, which manifests in the highest level of the mind - the *buddhi*. This pair, the divine ray and the ego, are like two angels, one good and the other bad. They accompany man on his spiritual journey, the one guiding and expanding him and the other impeding his progress, and they do not cease to operate within him until he has reached his goal and become a free being.

The different departments of learning, from the lowest to the highest, attract through their capacity to refine the mind and prepare it for its expansion, and they are indeed the vehicles of knowledge. The so-called higher mental activities, the arts and the sciences, are only considered to be high because they bring the higher reaches of the mind into play, and through this service alone they claim their devotees and their martyrs.

But an objection arises here. If the mind can be thus moulded and expanded, if it is an object and an instrument, then it cannot be the force which will lead man to freedom. There must be some other factor, an inner power, which impels and moulds the mind. Such a power must be cognisant of the end as well as the beginning, and is therefore outside time. It cannot be subject to natural laws; in other words, it must be timeless and changeless - a divine standard of measurement. As we have said, this power is held in the Vedanta philosophy to be a ray of the supreme

Consciousness, the *Atman*, and by virtue of its untouched reality it bestows an appearance of reality and existence on all phenomena.

If a ray of divine Consciousness does in fact lodge within man's mind, how is it that he does not fly, straight as a homing bird, to his goal? The rays emanating from the sun produce the cosmic food, so to say, which sustains life in all matter. Even when the sun is obscured from view, these rays still permeate the universe, giving this hidden food whereby everything lives. In the same way the supreme spirit produces the semblance of consciousness in phenomena. It is invisible and intangible, yet all subsist on it and exist by virtue of it. The ray of this spirit, which is reflected in the mind of man, is one with the great sun of *Atman* or God. It is the cause of the mind's restlessness and also of its capacity for transcendence and joy. But it is hidden, and if man is to know directly the supreme Consciousness from which this divine ray emanates, and become identified with it, he must first pass through and emerge from the temporal glamour which surrounds and at present obscures it, and which is like the brilliant and blinding light which prevents the eye from having a direct sight of the sun.

This power - this glamour - is called *maya* in the Vedanta philosophy. It is at once an emanation of the divine Lord and the cause of man's insufficiency of knowledge of Him, for not only does it blind him to ultimate perfection, but it distorts what he can see on the temporal plane. It is a subtle conception and worthy of deep consideration. Just as the luminosity surrounding the sun prevents the mortal eye from regarding it directly, so *maya* prevents the divinity underlying all objects from becoming apparent. It also invests those objects with attraction and a semblance of reality which does not rightly belong to them, as objects.

We have suggested that, in order to claim man's interest and devotion, any object of his attention must guarantee an opportunity for his expansion. But what does this divine science of Adhyatma Yoga have to teach us about expansion? Every day man is discovered, by those who should know, to be more and more complex. His mind is now held to be his own only in part. His thoughts and reactions are apparently not completely his own, nor what they appear to be. It is held that his emotions are most certainly not entirely his own. What will the poor thing be left with, which is his own, when the psychologists have done picking his bones?

Throughout the ages the spiritual schools or religions, and the secret sciences (called 'secret' because they can only reveal their findings to those who are attuned to them) have made pronouncements on this apparently poor creature, which are unanimous and definite. One is that man harbours an unknown continent within him. This continent is not synonymous with the sub-conscious of the psychologists. According to the knowers of Truth man will only begin to recognise his true status when he turns within and starts to explore it. Now this is a lure, for it promises him unknown expansion and experience. But in time he will have to pass beyond the frontiers of this country, just as he will have to pass beyond the confines of his conscious mind.

The second pronouncement made by these illumined sages or knowers, is that the deeper man penetrates into that inner continent, the more one-pointed and homogeneous does he become, until his need, his urgency, is reduced to one single motive - to know himself. This is synonymous with knowing God through the direct experience of identity.

Many will say: 'But surely this fixation on one point is a restriction; it cannot bring the joy of varied and universal experience.' Well, evidently the bee thinks it can! Buzzing anxiously about, he also is in search of one thing only - nectar - and when he finds its hiding place, he disappears into that flower and drinks long and in silence and, we imagine, in ecstasy. What man desires cannot be confined by the world of time and space, and yet it is contained in a single point.

It is all very well to make the assertion that man's highest need is to know himself or God, but can we prove this? This is a vital question, because if it cannot be met, then the Yoga will have failed, for the avenue of expansion promised will be closed. No-one calls for proof that the divine Consciousness or God exists, for this does not admit of mental proof. But we do seek for proof that there exists a state in man in which he can know this supreme Being directly, and by experience - if in fact it does exist. Proof is carried out by a finite instrument, the mind. It is a mental exercise performed on a mental concept. But the supra-mental does not come within the range of proof, for that is a region where the criterion of acceptance is experience, and experience of a very subtle and pure nature. It is inspirational and intuitional. The hallmark of this experience is certainty, and it is subscribed to spontaneously on all levels of consciousness. It makes itself known in the form of a remembrance, rather than a newly discovered fact.

The untrained man expects every happening and statement to be held in suspension until it has been acknowledged by his mind to be logically watertight. In other words, he expects to understand everything, finite and infinite, through his finite mind. This is a blunder of the first water, because minds suffer from rigidity, caused by long-held ideas and desires, from disappointments and shocks, which have assailed them over a long period. Therefore, as our Teacher used to say, after a certain stage we can only progress in understanding if we open up an extension to our finite mind and bring that into play. That extension will also have to give way to something higher, as the more subtle truths begin to reveal themselves. The progression is: mental enquiry and reason first, then the extension, inner experience, and finally the inspirational and intuitional power which interprets both.

We have now introduced two words into this description of expanding awareness - intuition and inspiration - and we have thereby introduced two very dangerous concepts. It is the universal testimony of those who have reached a high state of unfoldment, that the powers of inspiration and intuition do exist, but that they only emerge as active powers when the mind and its extension have reached the limit of their influence. Unfortunately the mind takes longer to reach its limit of operation than many believe. Desires, likes, dislikes, hopes and fears lurk within the mind long after it seems to have reached a quiescent and voided state. They come out again in the guise of inspiration and can reduce any situation to comedy, or make it appear as a tragedy. What is taken for inspiration at this stage is often egoistic invention masquerading as this high power.

When I was young I worked in a solicitor's office and we had two clients who were ardent and convinced

Buchmanites. At one point we had to prove their father's will, which turned out to be more complicated than had been expected. One day the firm received a letter from these two ladies. They said that during their silent hour, when God spoke to them and they interpreted what He had to say inspirationally, they had received the following message from Him: 'My children, you must leave that firm at once. They charge too much - the estate won't stand it.'

True inspirational power is purity itself and it requires a pure medium through which to operate. Man's mind - his instincts, his understanding, the mental atmosphere in which he lives, moves and has his being - is not pure, that is, if purity means to be finally free from admixture with foreign elements - to be without qualifications. The purification, training and expansion of the mind until it only acts when under the direction of these higher powers, is the purpose of the yogic discipline and meditation.

This training involves a voluntary and temporary restriction and direction of the mental activities, but its aim is the mastery of the mental instrument and the ultimate revelation of the great powers which lie behind it. In this respect, it is not different from any other training. To train for a running or hurdle race necessitates temporary physical restriction and short but progressive tests. The training of Yoga is more subtle, for it deals with a more subtle instrument than the body. But the point to remember is that, like all other training, it is, or should be, temporary. It has a term and it works towards a result. That result is complete and unbroken freedom through knowledge and inner experience.

If this idea is kept before the mind, it will create a

more positive attitude towards training, and will dispel
the erroneous idea that Yoga is a way of life. Yoga is
not a way of life, it is a way to life. The one who
practises it must always envisage his emergence from its
training rules into the life of a free being. There have
been many examples of this culmination of the yogic
training even in modern times, but these illumined ones
are not easily discovered and certainly not easily
recognised for what they are, even when found.

To return to the discipline. Just as in physical
training you look on the body as the instrument which
has to be manipulated and directed, so in the mental
training the mind must be objectively considered.
Before the investigator has studied the teachings of
Vedanta, he may think that although he can detach
himself from the body, it is not possible for him to
detach himself from the mind, in fact, that he must be
the mind. Even his way of speech encourages him in
this view: 'I am happy', 'I am angry', 'I am
miserable, but not so miserable as I was yesterday'.
But these pronouncements obviously come from some
inner and detached onlooker, present both today and
yesterday and therefore in a position to arbitrate
independently and with judgement between the strength
of the two emotions.

Here you will remember that it was said that the mind
was plastic and could be moulded. But it is certainly
not moulded by its ego, its complexes, its memories or
its emotions. They can push it about and have it under
duress, but they cannot mould and develop it. The
moulder is that ray of the divine spirit which dwells
within the mind.

You may say: 'But what about my heart and my
emotions, what about them? Won't I become as dry

as dust if I fix my attention on the mind alone?' Mind and heart, or rather their conscious reactions, emanate from and comprise one centre. When the emotional mode of the mind, called the *chitta* in Sanskrit, is awakened, we call it the heart, and where the scientific, critical and investigating mental mode is in the ascendant, it is called the mind. But the power which trains and transforms both levels will ultimately resolve everything into its own likeness - no, not into its likeness, but into itself, perfection; and its power lies in the fact that it is the only living - that means, the only *conscious* - element in man's organism.

Now it is certain that no-one will automatically accept this statement as truth. In order to satisfy himself whether it is truth or not, the enquirer must seek out a Centre, a source of information which he feels he can trust to give him the traditional teachings in a pure and classical form. He should remain there for some time, receiving the Truth as given there, and he should also learn to exercise the spiritual quality which is known in the philosophy as enquiry or *vichara*.

Enquiry and investigation are not two names for the same mental activity. Investigation calls up the critical faculty and already acquired knowledge, but enquiry starts with no pre-conceived ideas. It receives, one might almost say, through the ear and not through the mind, and it listens with unbiassed attention to whatever is offered. At first it receives and that is all. It does not analyse what it receives, but takes it in as a whole, opening the mind to its impact.

This is not the stage at which questions such as 'Is it true?', 'Is it workable?' arise. At first the enquirer must be like stout Cortez, the explorer in Keats' sonnet. The poet tells us how he stared with eagle eyes at the Pacific while his men stood round him, gazing at it in silence. He did not immediately consult his chart and compass, or argue with his crew as to whether this could be what they were seeking. Together they stared at the ocean in silence, taking it in. This is what is meant by enquiry. Ideas, like people, have an atmosphere which surrounds them and is individual to them. They can only be transmitted to those who approach them unarmed. Later the details of the atmosphere will be better known and assessed, and then it will not be sensed so strongly! Now is the time to savour what it really has to offer as its gift, and to be subtly changed by it.

In the yogic training this enquiry is divided into three progressive stages. The first stage is *shravana*. This is the hearing and receiving, which has been described. It is followed by *manana*, or brooding on what has been imparted and critically assessing it. Lastly there is *nididhyasana*, or meditating on it.

Shravana is rather like reading or hearing a pronouncement for the first time, which is to have great importance for you, and then relating it to yourself. It is like catching at the meaning of a whole sentence and not getting entangled with the individual words. On the other hand, *manana* involves going over this sentence or pronouncement word by word and considering their individual meaning and their value in the sentence. This is performed with the constructive, and not the destructive, critical faculty. *Nididhyasana* is the state of meditation, where once more the critical faculty is discarded. The meaning of the sentence or pronouncement is at last affirmed.

You must first find some place where the Truth is still presented without compromise and as nearly as possible as it was first given by the illumined sages. Then you must feed your mind's hunger by receiving what is offered in a spirit of acceptance. After this the concepts are presented for critical consideration by your mind, and thus for their final acceptance or rejection. All the time, the attention of the enquirer will be playing round the subject as a whole and, if it is not discarded as unworthy of further investigation, his preoccupation with it will deepen, until he gets his first experience of meditation. Now he will cease to wonder whether it be true, he will affirm that it is so, and the power of his affirmation will lead him deeper and deeper into the flower of Truth, like the bee, until at last he knows its perfection by the direct experience of tasting its nectar.

You may think: 'I shall never find time to attempt study, what to say of meditation.' But a Zen master has said: 'If you really mean to do it, you can. You can always find five minutes for quiet even in the midst of affairs. By this five minutes' margin nearly everything can be solved.' And again he says: 'The real rest is not rest in rest, but rest in activity. Likewise, meditation in activity is a hundred, a thousand, a million times superior to meditation in repose.' Here he affirms, as did our Teacher, that in the end we must be able to carry out all spiritual activities in the midst of the worldly activities.

IX

CONSERVATION OF ENERGY

THE CONSERVATION of energy may perhaps seem
too practical a subject to have any spiritual significance. But here, straight away, we come on one of the
principal tenets of the philosophy of non-dualism,
namely, that there is nothing whatsoever which does
not have some spiritual import. Everything which can
be apprehended through the mind or the senses is
interpenetrated by Consciousness or chit, and is made
knowable and exhibits its particular qualities by virtue
of that Consciousness.

Anyone who wishes to grasp the philosophy on which
Adhyatma Yoga is based will be faced at once with the
inadequacy of this term 'Consciousness'. It is used to
denote that power, one-without-a-second, which
contains within itself the basic facts, known in this
empirical realm as existence, being, bliss and fullness.
This chit, or the supreme reality, is the germ of all
apparent reality in phenomena. It is unimaginable,
unchangeable and all-pervading, and it is that which
invests the universe of names and forms with its
apparent power, movement, beauty and evanescence,
while remaining itself unchanged in the process.

The appearance of names and forms within this all-
pervading formless chit, is held to be the visible result
of a power inherent in it called maya, composed of
three degrees of activity and density known as the three
gunas. This power of maya, together with the three
gunas, veils the light of chit; it is also postulated in the

Advaita philosophy as the cause of the empirical world.

Maya is immaterial and inexplicable. It conceals the nature of reality by causing the infinite to appear as finite. It produces the conception of time and space, where in reality there exists only the unbroken stretch of Consciousness. All manifestations of power spring from this one source - *chit* - seen through the distorting medium of the power of *maya* and its three *gunas*. This causes its power to manifest in the empirical world as energy, its *being* as the phenomenon of life, and its *bliss* as human love and worldly attraction.

One would think that this reality, so powerful and all-comprising, could never be hidden, that it must necessarily reveal itself in its entirety to the empirical consciousness of man and not appear as if made up of parts and effects. But it must be remembered that man is himself a part of this *mayic* perversion or delusion so far as his body and mind are concerned, and therefore blind to reality, for though the sea may know the wave, the wave will never recognise the mighty ocean until it becomes one with it.

The sun's rays are all-pervading and its naked light cannot be borne by the human eye, and yet a leaf held before the face can block its brilliance from view. Empirical existence, with its conception of multiplicity, time, space, forms, concepts and percepts, is as a leaf held before the divine vision. The end and aim of conscious spiritual endeavour is to remove this obstruction and, seeing Truth in its fullness, to recognise it as the basic nature of all things and re-enter it, finally and for ever. It will thus be seen that Yoga is really a process of unlearning, of readjustment and removal, rather than a science which will impart something new to the learner. This is borne out by the fact that at each progressive stage in his training the pupil seems to recognise the country he is entering and his sense of security and joy increases as he proceeds.

These words may give a general idea of the goal of the spiritual endeavour, but our interest is to see how the power of God, or reality, which permeates all, may be loosed from the restrictions created by the illusion of *maya*, and so manifest in its fullness.

Power and energy are obviously not one and the same thing. Energy is the outcome of the action of power on an object. The magnet - itself immobile and without qualities - creates a manifestation of intense energy and movement in the iron filings which come within its orbit, but is itself untouched and unchanged. The question before us is not how to conserve power, for that will never change in quality or intensity, but how to manipulate the object upon which this power plays - in this case the body and mind - in such a way that they may be filled with energy and retain it for as long as possible; that is the problem.

Some may wonder how that which is greater can be manipulated by that which is less - in other words, how such a power can be turned to man's uses, and apparently undergo a change, when conceived by the mind. Our Teacher used to explain this by using the simile of a glacier, rising high up in the Himalayan heights, where its waters are pure and uncontaminated. The water descends to join the rivers of the plains on their way to the sea, and in its progress it passes through many cities where the inhabitants throw their refuse into it. The water has now become turbid and polluted, and yet it is the same element which issued from the glacier far away on the Himalayan peaks. The change has been wrought by the action of man alone, and is temporary, for it will pass away when the water reaches the infinite ocean. Just so chit - Consciousness - or whatever you wish to call it, interpenetrates all phenomena. But due to the finitising power of maya, it is seen everywhere as the pairs of opposites - as terror as well as joy, hatred as well as bliss. It is the same force or element which makes the sun shine, the atoms cohere and at the same time causes man to think, have likes and dislikes and create a battleground of moods and emotions within his mind. And yet this Consciousness is intrinsically without form, limits or qualities.

Granted that this is so, how is it possible to call a halt and resume one's own nature, which is one with this pure element? What steps are to be taken to withdraw the leaf from before the inner eye, so that its vision may be unobstructed and undistorted? The world is suffering from universal tension. Wars and rumours of wars, not to speak of personal discord and fears, are taking an enormous toll of our mental and nervous energy. Something must be done by each individual to stop this waste and to bring the nerves and mind into a state of equilibrium, in which they are not so easily affected by the adversities of life. This is the value of the practices of Yoga and the facts on which they are based.

According to the Vedanta, before man becomes self-conscious, that is, before he conceives of himself as other than the body and the mind, and superior to both, he is like a web, made up of the mind and its contents and the body and its reactions, though both are animated by the divine spirit. The body and mind have no power of activity in themselves, but are energised and made seemingly alive through their proximity with Consciousness. It is held that through creation, that is, wherever the power of maya reaches - and it is all-pervasive - the light of Consciousness is veiled by three densities or impulses towards activity, known as the three gunas. It might be said that maya is another name for these three gunas and the gunas are another name for maya. These gunas condition the reception of chit by an object; they are known as tamas, rajas and sattva and are present in varying degrees in all phenomena.

Tamas is the guna which produces the thickest veil. It manifests as the inertness in matter, and as error, sloth and the absence of discrimination in the mind. Rajas produces a less complete veiling; it is the principle of activity, manifesting as life in all things, and desire, greed and ambition in the mind. Sattva produces the most subtle veil; it is the principle of transparency and reflection, and gives rise to the qualities of balance and understanding in the mind. The gunas are said to act together and they form the changing texture of the outer and inner life. They are all present in matter, mind and life, but each in varying degree. Thus, although tamas predominates in matter, the sattva guna, the principle which reflects or manifests Consciousness most clearly, is present there also.

Therefore Consciousness is not only present, but is faintly discernible even in the lowest forms of matter - a fact which has now been established by science. Matter is resistant, for it has the tamas guna predominating, but although it may appear stable to the eye, its every particle - atoms and molecules - is capable of change and motion. In other words rajas is present. There is also rhythm in this movement, indicating the presence of sattva.

As in matter, so in man. He also is an admixture, not a simple product, all three *gunas* being present in him. But in man they are subject to alternation, one *guna* gaining the ascendancy at one time and another at another, and this alternation persists until he achieves inner control. Therefore he has no reason for hopelessness, nor complacency for that matter. For he will never be safe from the pitching and tossing of the three *gunas* until he has reached his natural state, that is, until their influence has been neutralised and transcended.

At this point one asks oneself: 'Is there a purpose in this perpetual exchange?' According to Vachaspati Misra, an early philosopher of Vedanta, there is a purpose, for he has written:

Like a lamp, the action of the *gunas* is for a single purpose. The wick and the oil in a lamp are each, by themselves, opposed to the action of fire, but they co-operate when in contact with fire for the single purpose of giving light. The various humours of the body, though possessed of contradictory properties, co-operate for the single purpose of sustaining the body. In the same manner, the three *gunas*, though possessed of mutually contradictory properties, co-operate towards a single end - the emancipation of the spirit.

That is to say, the *gunas*, through their very existence and activity, drive man to transcend them and so to win his freedom.

How does this emancipation take place? The true nature of man is complete freedom and sovereignty, and he will never be satisfied until he has unveiled his

96

nature and lives in it. He will therefore be impelled at long last to free himself from any domination or restriction whatsoever. The most complete domination is servitude to the influence of the *gunas*, whereas liberty means their transcendence. Spiritual training, discipline and instruction have this emancipation as their goal. The progression they teach is from the domination of *tamas* to the ascendancy of *sattva* and then beyond that.

There is much instruction in the *Bhagavad Gita* on how to transcend the *gunas*, and so to control mental activity which leads to bodily action, and also on how to conserve energy. In one verse it says:

The *gunas* perform all action. With understanding deluded, the ignorant man thinks 'I am the doer'.

This verse is often tortured into meaning: 'I am not responsible for my actions, for it is the *gunas* that are acting.' But nothing in this world is as simple as that! We are responsible, in so far as we offer the suitable soil in which a specific *guna* can flourish and in which a certain type of action can germinate and bear fruit.

Yet the true position is implied in this *Gita* verse. It is the ignorant man who identifies himself with the automatic activity which is brought about by the *gunas*. It is the attraction of the *gunas* to each other that causes action and therefore reaction. They cause reactions in the subtle senses and responses in the gross body. The true Self is detached from the senses, the mind and - in the end - from the *gunas* as well. But only when this fact has been confirmed by direct experience and therefore has become an ever-present certainty, to be acted upon automatically, has the man earned the right to dissociate himself from his actions and reactions. By that time the false self will have become as incapable of doing harm as a snake with its poison fangs removed. He will not reach this state of transcendence by abstaining from action, but by dispassionately performing whatever action comes his way unsought.

How may a man free himself from this domination of the *gunas* and attain an altitude from where he can enjoy them, while remaining untouched by their machinations? There is an Eastern saying: 'While the pearl is still in the oyster it cannot decorate the royal crown.' So long as we are netted down and in thrall to anything, our true nature will be hidden and we shall be in bondage. Balance, so long as it is consciously maintained, still contains within itself the seed of the fear of falling. It needs courage to maintain a balance, but fearlessness only comes to him whose feet are both firmly planted on the ground.

Different aspects of the training provide different means of controlling the *gunas*, and stopping the ceaseless squandering of energy they bring about. These practices are directed at the heart or the intuitional centre, the mind and the will. In each case they aim at slowing down unbridled activity, through conscious and enlightened selection, thereby allowing the power behind these centres to manifest.

Meditation, control of the mind and alertness or concentration - these are the practices. Meditation empties the heart of temporal concepts and then fills it with the infinite and abstract. True control of the mind means discovering and controlling the cause of its activity and not only controlling the effect - the activity in itself. The cause will only be revealed through intuition, born of meditation, but its effects may be neutralised through control of the damaging mental wastage caused by unpremeditated speech and the idle imaginings born of desire and aversion. Finally, concentration on a focus is practised, which alone makes the sustaining of the *sattva guna* possible. These practices produce a technique which teaches the pupil how to rise above those causes of ignorance - the *gunas*.

There is a passage in the *Masnavi* of Rumi where the perfect way of robbing the *gunas* of their power to distract and steal is given:

O God, there are myriads of snares and baits and we are greedy foolish birds, O Thou without want! We are putting corn into our barn and yet we are losing the corn that has been garnered. If there were no thievish mice in our barn, where is the corn of forty years of devotion? Why is the daily sincerity of our devotion not being stored in this barn of ours? But though there be a thousand snares at our feet, if Thou art with us there will be no trouble.

That is the secret: 'If Thou art with us, there will be no trouble.' So long as we keep our heart's eye on God or Truth, these snares - these shifting *gunas* - will have no power to rob us.

So it seems that the power of the *gunas* can only be broken when something greater than they are swims into our view and is acknowledged by our mind. The Lord in the *Gita* says: 'Verily this divine illusion of mine, made up of the *gunas*, is hard to surmount. Only those who devote themselves to Me alone cross over it.' The secret thieves of energy are the *gunas*. The only way of preserving our treasure is to dissociate ourselves from them, by transferring our inner gaze to the Unchanging, and merely witnessing their changing activities without being influenced by them.

Dr. Shastri used to say: 'Imagine a certain volume of water. If that water is confined within banks, that is to say, if it is conserved and directed to its proper course towards the sea, it will become a deep moving stream. But allow it to spread unrestricted over a two acre field, and it will only be a few inches in depth, have no movement, and will soon become stagnant.' Control and direction are the methods to be employed if energy is to be conserved and the supreme Truth known.

The final verdict of the Upanishadic sages is: 'No-one whose senses are unpurified and whose mind is not collected and at rest, can acquire knowledge of the Self.' The only certain way to release is withdrawal from the endless experiences of the senses and the mind, and concentration through meditation on the subtle realm behind and above the mind.

In fact, the saints of all religions have proved this by their lives. They are manifestations of extreme yet selective energy, which is apparently inexhaustible. They draw the spiritual power naturally through the now open and purified channels of their hearts and minds, and they conserve it by devoting it exclusively to the glory and service of the source from which it comes, and with which they are now consciously joined. To them, the whole world and their bodies and minds as well, are manifestations of this Power, and their lives are dedicated to revealing this Truth to others. The more directly the fact of the all-pervadingness of God is realised by them, the more clearly will it reveal itself to their fellow men. For man can only take fire from a living flame and not by contact with the dry sticks of theories.

This may be so, but we are not saints. We have still to bring this Truth into being for ourselves in this world, and there are certain outer ways of doing so. Among these is the elimination of unnecessary activity on all planes. First and foremost amongst those activities is the habit of unconsidered and exuberant speech, which is like a tap with a perished washer, allowing the water constantly to run to waste. There is an old saying that every man is allotted, at his birth, just so many breaths and no more. If he excites himself or allows himself to become angry or voluble, his breath quickens and he spends it recklessly and to no purpose. He is therefore forced to leave the stage of life before his due time. This may be a cri de coeur from some monosyllabic one, linked to a voluble talker, but it has a value as a warning all the same.

After having started to curb his outgoing activities, the disciple must establish a rhythm and formulate a plan by which to live his daily life. This will prevent preoccupation with trifles and make it possible for the mind to turn to essentials. Order without is generally an indication of order within, and this powerful practice of selection and rejection must be mastered if man is to be able to direct his life, instead of allowing it to direct him.

The two inner practices of meditation and contemplation make these outer ones fruitful, and also - and this must never be forgotten - the cultivation of a universal outlook which will not countenance harm to any by thought, word or deed. Where this attitude is not present, it means that there is an absence of the true understanding of the Advaita philosophy and, what is more serious, no belief in the all-pervadingness of spirit.

Withdrawal from the surface life in order to concentrate on its substratum - the Unmanifest - through the study of meditation and contemplation, together with this feeling of universal goodwill, are the traditional methods for conserving spiritual power and energy.

One short verse of Shri Shankara tells us that true freedom means freedom of action on this plane of being as well as on the highest:

> One may live the life of the world or be a monk, live in society or in a hermitage, but he whose mind is devoted to the joy of the contemplation of God, he is happy, he is happy, he is happy.

It is only by ceasing to roam that a man reaches the inexhaustible within his own nature, and by identifying himself with the One that he escapes domination by the many.

X

DEPENDENCE AND INDEPENDENCE

IN DR SHASTRI'S free translation of the *Gita*, published as *Teachings from the Bhagavad Gita*, it is said: 'Those who disregard the spiritual experience of the sages of the past, and act according to their own impulses, thinking they can follow Yoga and meditation independently, fail to obtain happiness, perfection and the supreme goal.' He adds the comment: 'Personal guidance is essential to perfection in Yoga. One must always ponder on the experience of the sages, as recorded in the scriptures, and follow the rules of ethics laid down by them, and the discipline which they prescribe. It is foolish for a man to say "I follow my own path", misinterpreting his emotions as intuitions.'

There is a verse in the Upanishads which says something to this effect: 'Rare is the true Teacher and rarer still is the true pupil, but where this rare partnership is present, anything may be achieved.' In the verse from the *Gita*, the dependence of the pupil on his Teacher is implied and advocated. This dependence has nothing to do with servitude or servility. It is a voluntary state which will ultimately be transcended, just as every other phase of the inner training, and in fact every phase of life too, will have to be transcended if the goal is to be reached.

Even Yoga itself, if it is considered as an end and not as a means to an end, will prove static and unproductive. Yoga is not a way of life; it is a preparation for the true and free life and only *that*.

When its object has been gained, it can be laid aside. The illumined yogi does not need to practise it any more. He lives it, and henceforth he will make no mistakes and harm none.

Dr Shastri was a very great Teacher indeed, and his pupils were fortunate enough to be given some experience of the practical implication of the words quoted. But the West does not take very kindly to the idea of dependence, which is regarded as a sign of weakness or superficial acceptance, and in the beginning many of us thought the same. We felt that our prejudices were not really prejudices at all, but reasoned convictions, and that the conventionality which was strong in some of us was, in fact, integrity. It was only after much water had passed under our bridges that the idea began to dawn on some of us that we were not being offered a new science or system of thought, that is, an intellectual adventure. We were being given a spiritual opportunity in the form of a particular and tested way of unveiling Truth.

Truth is revealed in its entirety to illumined men alone, but a faint surmise of its existence lies hidden in every heart, and it lures men on to many adventures. The method by which it is disclosed can be imparted only by those who have already been successful in the search, for it is highly specialised and calls for the dedication of heart and mind rather than a rearrangement of the worldly circumstances.

Dr Shastri once said that all knowledge has one object and it is the bringing into view, the pursuit and finally the capture of its quarry - Truth; and that knowledge is at root one. The knowledge by which a human being is known is basically the same as that by which God is known. The sphere of its operation is different, but the consciousness which plays on it is the same.

Perhaps the chief work of Dr Shastri's literary life was the translation of *The Ramayana of Valmiki*. This is a tremendous epic of thousands of *slokas*, and in it there is a story of a magic deer which lures Prince Rama away from his hermitage into the forest. Changing its shape and colour at will, it entices him further and further into the trees. Truth is like that deer, insofar as every desire which attracts man is Truth under some disguise. Its pursuit is the motive of life here on earth, and anyone who says that it is only exercise that a sportsman is after has never felt the magic of the chase. Yoga, like all other enterprises, is intended to reach an objective, and when that has been gained, you can dismount from your horse and sit in the shade.

At this point a questioner may say: 'I have no use for similes; what I want to know is how a man is to decide what he will pursue and study and what will really suit him. Surely he must use the knowledge he already has of himself to guide him? What is the use of placing trust in someone who has probably only just come into his life and who cannot know his psychological difficulties so soon?'

The answer to this query, or objection, is that the last thing a man will come to know is himself. At the start he is too deeply implicated in trying to interpret his various reactions, and with his sense of inferiority or superiority, to be able to form any true estimate of himself. All he can usually produce at this stage is a despairing sigh - not a verdict. Due to this almost inevitable preoccupation with himself, his assessment of the world of ideas and things around him is faulty and coloured by the ego sense.

But those who have stepped outside themselves - the illumined Teachers - see differently. They have brought those great powers which, in an ordinary man, lie unsuspected behind his active mind, into the foreground and into focus. To the Teachers, every man is a spiritual embryo and not an already completed human being, and they are quite sure of the glories which await him. It is through the hidden transference of their concentrated creative vision of man's destiny that inner changes are set up in him, and these changes will at long last bring him the freedom which they already enjoy. This freedom - this state of independence - is the goal of all endeavour and the unacknowledged desire of all men. But it is only achieved and earned by passing through a preliminary stage of pupilhood, which is synonymous with extreme dependence and a willingness to sacrifice the child of our own creation, our egoistic minds.

The Teachers of old used to be called *tirtha karas* or 'ford finders' - that is, those who knew the safe place to cross a river and who could therefore lead their followers through the dangerous currents of life. These 'ford finders' expected implicit obedience from the pilgrims in their band, if they were to bring them safely across the currents to the other shore. They had strong ideas of how a pupil should conduct himself while they were instructing him. They expected him to keep himself free from worldly influences, and in the *Maitri Upanishad* it describes some of the impediments to the acquirement of knowledge, which are the result of indiscriminate associationship with the worldly:

This is indeed the source of the net of delusion: associationship by one who is worthy of heaven with those who are not worthy of heaven - this is it! Now there are some who are always hilarious, always abroad, always begging. Though they are told there is a grove beside them, they cling to a small shrub. And others there are who are beggars in towns, who perform sacrifices for the unworthy, who are wicked, who wear their hair in a twisted knot, who are dancers, mercenaries, travelling mendicants, actors and those who have been degraded in the King's service. And others there are who for money profess that they can allay the evil influences of *yakshas*, *rakshasas*, ghosts, goblins, devils, serpents, imps and the like. And others there are who love to distract the believers in the Vedas by the jugglery of false arguments and comparisons - with them one should not associate. These creatures are evidently thieves and unworthy of heaven. For thus it has been said: The world, bewildered by the doctrines which deny the Self, by false comparisons and proofs, does not discern the difference between wisdom and knowledge.

Well, this makes our times seem quite dull and almost safe, but one still recognises some of the types! When you read such a catalogue of what was apparently considered attractive and tempting, one thinks of the writer who said: 'Distraction is the only thing that consoles us for our miseries, and yet it is itself the greatest of our miseries.'

These injunctions apply only to the accepted disciple, and then only while he is being trained. Later on he will be able to consort with whomsoever he pleases, for by that time he will be insulated, so to say. But there will always be those whose purpose sways about like a rocking cradle, who, as the *Maitri Upanishad* puts it, 'though told that there is a grove beside them, still cling to a small shrub'. These men must go their ways. But where the desire to know is coupled with a willingness to make sacrifices in order to know, and a determination to fulfil the requirements of the one who does know, progress is assured.

Dr Shastri used to say that power comes from obedience, when it is consciously and willingly practised, and that the pupil needed three things if he was to draw from the Teacher as a calf draws from the cow: a strong will, a strong faith and a programme. He once went so far as to say that you must be strong before you can be spiritual. The pupil will need a strong will to carry out intelligently the orders given by his Teacher. He will need a strong faith in the Truth and the ability of the Teacher to impart it. This faith, you may be sure, will be called into operation when the purposes of the Teacher are shrouded in mystery. A constructive plan makes the way easier for both the pupil and his Teacher. The pupil must think out this plan for himself, for even while he is dependent on the Teacher he must do certain things for himself. He will have to destroy his own pain by his own efforts, which means that he will have to put the teachings he is given into practice consciously, and not wait supine for everything to be done for him.

There is one other thing which he can do for himself. It is an imaginative exercise, which will make his path much smoother. He can visualise, which is a fact, that he lives in the body and mind and not *as* the body and mind - that he lives in the body as a guest or a lodger. No-one feels humiliated if his car is taken to pieces in the public highway to detect a fault, and no-one should be personally abased when imperfections in the personality are pointed out by the Teacher and he is told to remedy them. The mind is man's vehicle and not himself.

In all progress there is a time when, although growth is going on, it is hidden - it has gone underground, so to say. The winter fields look dead at a certain time of the year and so does the pupil, at certain stages in his training, and so does he feel. When this winter descends on him, he will need all his faith and courage to believe that this is pre-eminently a period when secret growth is going on, and that time and the warmth and rain of the Teacher's compassion will surely produce buds and shoots in his inner being in due course.

Now that the word 'time' has been mentioned, it must be considered. Our questioner is, we feel sure, used to the synthetic living of today, where to want is to have, or apparently to have, and then cease to have, as quickly; where concordances take the place of laborious but rewarding research, and radio and television administer pills of culture indiscriminately to all and sundry. He will no doubt say: 'Surely, this process of learning need not take so long as all that! It obviously could be speeded up with advantage, and will have to be, if it is to be of any use in this life.'

Unfortunately it is not so simple as that. It is not speedy to make lasting changes within and without, and the Eastern teaching has always been that you do not get wisdom by improving your mental faculties, but by purifying them. If you accept this, then you are in for a long and arduous business. Dr Shastri used to say that a cat has nine lives but the mind has nine hundred and more! The fact that the Truth which has been imparted by the Teacher has been grasped by the mind, is no evidence that it has been absorbed into the inner being. That will only be known by results.

To the Gurus of old and the true Teachers of today also, time, from one point of view, is of little account, but from another, it is looked on as the maturing factor. Wine can be drunk the year it is bottled, and to those who do not know what wine can be, it may be a treat, but to the connoisseur it will be a tragedy. Mellowness does not fall like dew from heaven: it rises from the root and spreads through the whole organism. The yogic instructors knew that need, long felt, fosters imagination and intensity, and ripens the personality. It was part of their technique to place obstacles in the path of the disciple in order to increase this need and test his determination to hold on.

The Upanishads are full of tales of Teachers who kept their disciples apparently idle for years, watching the desired instruction being given to others. We can imagine that those whose purpose was weak soon passed from the scene with imprecations. But when the moment for direct instruction of the true pupil arrived, he would learn in a flash, for the ground of his mind had been purified and matured during that long period of waiting, obedience and service.

The importance of the time factor in training and the impossibility of hurry is a point which is stressed in many of the classics. The great Dattatreya says in the *Avadhut Gita*: 'This *Atman* of which the high yogis speak, most subtle, beyond perception, without attributes, must be realised step by step, and not by sudden violence.' In the *Maitri Upanishad* there is a beautiful description of the disciple at the moment when he passes from dependence to independence:

Having left behind (that is, forgotten or trans-cended) the elements, the objects of the senses and the organs of sense, and having seized the bow whose stick is fortitude and whose string is asceticism, and having struck down the first guardian at the door of *Brahma* with the arrow which is fashioned of freedom from egoism, he crosses, by means of the boat OM, to the other side of the space within the heart and slowly enters into the hall of *Brahma*, as a miner seeking minerals enters into a mine. After that, let him by means of the doctrine of his Teacher, break through the shrine of *Brahma* and reach the last shrine, that of blessedness and identity with *Brahman*. Now he has gained his independence. Henceforth, pure, tranquil, imperishable, firm and independent, he abides in his own greatness and looks down on the wheel of the world as one who has alighted from a chariot looks on its revolving wheels.

When this stage is reached, there is no dependence on control of the mind, or indeed on control of any kind. The peak of being is independence of all external and internal things. It is in a sense self-dependence, but the self is then the Self of all.

By now our questioner, who is, as we know, given to interruptions, has been shifting in his seat for some time and he breaks in with a contribution. 'Very beautiful indeed', he says, 'but suppose there is no Teacher available to instruct and to be served and to be depended on? Surely the whole thing doesn't make sense without one?'

This is his trump card, so let him play it! The poor

man is evidently very modern and a worshipper of time and speed, but we have already proved that we are building for eternity and not erecting a dwelling like a modern house, which will be swept away before we are. The masters of any art are not easy of access, and very often they require the potential pupil to pass through other hands before they consent to teach him themselves. The pupil is not born on the day he is accepted by a Teacher. He is born on the day on which he starts preparing for a Teacher.

When I was young I studied the piano in Germany and, due to an error, I was accepted by a very great teacher indeed. But what a lot of unnecessary work he had to do because through this mistake I had come to him direct, too soon and not properly prepared. 'You should have done all this before you came to me', he used to grumble, and I suffered proportionately. The consciously held purpose is everything, from first to last. Once you work with a clearly defined objective in view, and are willing to wait and to sacrifice in order to achieve your purpose, events will fall into place and you will get your Teacher in his own good time. During the period of so-called waiting, which is really a period of inner preparation, there is a lot that can be done.

The inner qualities such as patience, continuity of purpose and courage, have to be awakened and fostered. I remember Dr Shastri once telling a potential pupil whom he had not yet finally accepted, that he should meditate every day on some virtue such as forgiveness, angerlessness, fortitude and so forth, and that when he had come to the end of the list, he should go over it again! Without a bowing acquaintance with these virtues, there can be no control of the mind or the emotions, and without control, there will be no entry

nto the realm of meditation. Dr Shastri also advised
spirants to read about the saints of God of all lands,
romising that holiness would pass into them while they
ead. This must be so, for the great ones keep nothing
or themselves. Even with his pupils, Dr Shastri's test
f whether you had absorbed some teaching into your
ystem, was whether you practised it and manifested it
n such a way that others fell in love with it, and
dopted it without knowing why.

Surely our questioner will now agree that there is
lenty to do before the actual training by a recognised
eacher begins. In the great classics such as the
Bhagavad Gita and the *Viveka-Chudamani (Crest
ewel of Wisdom)*, and also in the works of Swami
Rama Tirtha and our Teacher, a great many valuable
ints are given which will help the aspirant at this
tage. He must foster his spirit of enquiry by study,
ssociation with those who know, and constructive
uestioning.

Truth can come from many unexpected sources. It
an come from the north, south, east and west, and the
ne who imparts it need not necessarily be a human
eing. The important point for the would-be learner is
o keep alert and alive and, above all, unprejudiced, so
hat he may recognise instruction when it appears.

In the *Shrimad Bhagavatam* the great sage Dattatreya
estifies that he has learnt from many Teachers, not
nly one. He says that he has been instructed, amongst
thers, by water, by the earth, by the wind, by the
ea, by the arrow-maker:

> As water is sweet and pure, from it I have learnt
> the good taste of tastelessness. I have therefore
> taken water as one of my Gurus. Patience,

forgiveness, supporting others without expectation of gratitude, this I have learnt from my Guru the earth. The wind blows everywhere, over the flower-beds, deserts, marshes, palaces and prisons, without being attached to any of them, without preference or dislike. So I go everywhere scattering my blessings of peace, without being attached to anyone. My Guru the wind has taught me this lesson.

Though thousands of rivers empty themselves into the sea and yet it remains within its limits, so remains undisturbed the mind of the knower of God, though objects of all kinds pour themselves into it. Thus is the sea my Guru.

From the arrow-maker I have learnt the value of concentration. In a certain town there lived an arrow-maker who devoted his full attention to his trade. Once while he was beating the point of an arrow, the King and his procession went by in the street. He was so attentive to his work that he knew nothing of the King's passing, and when they asked him how he liked the music of the procession he asked: 'What procession? When did it pass?' So ought we to concentrate on Truth, so that no external object or event can disturb us.

This extract was translated by Dr Shastri, and he also translated the *Avadhut Gita*, which is the song of this great sage. Surely it shows that there are many sources of instruction and inspiration to be tapped before we need despair of attracting the attention of a holy Teacher.

XI

GRASPING THE ESSENTIALS

SPIRITUAL awakening to peace and transcendence is likely to be, relatively, an even longer drawn out affair than is our daily awakening to the turmoil of life. To be fully awake is no small achievement. Our Teacher used to tell us that only a very few men manage to become even sixty per cent alive before they die, but that those who do become fully conscious, develop qualities, asleep in the ordinary man, which can turn them into spiritual sages and Teachers.

This talk is on grasping the essentials, so it will only deal with a section of the process of waking, so to say - with the preliminary stage - that is, when a man passes from one state of consciousness to another and begins to experiment on what he had best to do to get himself up and broad awake.

Most of us know, to our shame, that our daily rising is not a very edifying spectacle, being in most cases a half-conscious battle between will and inclination. 'John', calls the eternal mother to the eternal child, 'get up at once, this is the third time I've been up to call you.' 'It's no good being angry with me, it's the sheets - they're holding me down.' So he says, and so he believes. And so do we, grown-up children, apparently believe also, for we countenance an unholy alliance between ourselves and circumstances and desires, which after all are the grown-up equivalent of sheets and blankets. But things can be speeded up. An alarm clock in the form of some outer agency can shake us awake; the anticipation of some important happening to come can also rouse us; or, best of all, the will can be trained to deal with the situation. But whichever way is chosen, it calls for some degree of decision and direct action on our part.

Yet this is a surface truth only. There is a basic reason which causes man to open his eyes and a motive power which can drive him before it either to heaven or hell. It is the necessity to experience - to experiment and then to experience the results of those experiments.

From this it might be inferred that man is on an aimless, never-ending search for stimulus. But the teaching of all the eastern spiritual schools, including Yoga, is just the reverse. Man is said to be on a self-imposed search for the end of experience, for that state which allows of no further expansion and therefore of no further experience either. Although in his present state he apparently revels in multiplicity and variety and the reactions they evoke in him, man is in fact searching for the opposite condition. He is searching not for a passing state of experience but for security, complete satisfaction, and a state of being which will embrace and stabilise his whole nature, finally and for ever.

The teaching of the Vedanta is that all phenomena - all concepts and percepts, all in fact that has name and form and is seemingly real and permanent at the first impact - is revealed as impermanent when compared with some more fundamental concept such as time and space. These wider concepts are again discovered, in their turn, to be illusory and passing when viewed against the unchanging and eternal Fact which lies behind them all. This is the fact of pure Consciousness - the One-without-a-second. In this way multiplicity, of which man himself is a part, dissolves inevitably into unity - into waveless being. In the last analysis, the whole universe is held to be pure Consciousness - that and that alone. Man will neither rest nor experience the bliss which forms the basis of his nature until he is tired of endless acquiring and relinquishing. It is only when he transcends the apparent convolutions of consciousness which are registered through the empirical mind, that he will come to rest in the peace and bliss which form the true centre of his being.

This statement will probably be repudiated by the seeker at first, for he regards the absence of action and reaction as synonymous with the absence of growth, and he is seeking growth at this stage - not knowledge as yet, but growth and expansion. But if he tests the teachings and begins his climb, he will find at a certain point that he is apparently coming under the direction of some law. The outer manifestation of this law is a sense of restlessness. He is conscious of a want of finality when the experiments he makes are connected with his individual progress and interests alone. On the other hand, he feels a faint sense of satisfaction whenever he attempts to universalise those interests.

This moment marks his first recognition of the spiritual and universal law, called in Sanskrit the law of *dharma*. This law, once recognised, however dimly, cannot be broken with impunity. In fact it cannot be called a law in the ordinary sense of the word, for it reveals and furthers the working out in *sansara* (worldly life) of the instinct, conscious or otherwise, to transcend the sense of separation and to recognise oneness with the whole. In other words, *dharma* furthers the instinct in all things to coalesce, to draw together and to universalise.

117

Victor Hugo said that love means the reduction of the universe to a single being and the expansion of that single being even to God. This statement bears a strong resemblance to the philosophical truth of non-duality, where the universe is reduced to one single unit of Consciousness and man is seen to be no other than that divine Consciousness itself. The practical implications of this truth, and man's acknowledgement of them, form the motive power of the law of dharma. We know that in his poem Victor Hugo was speaking of worldly love, but that love provides one of the ways by which man may recognise his capacity to transcend the boundaries of his personality and lose himself in unity. This recognition foreshadows his final condition.

How to strengthen this latent sense of greatness in man, and yet increase his obedience to the law of dharma (benevolence or righteousness) - this is the purpose of the training of Yoga. The Yoga is itself based on the law of dharma or the truth of universal brotherhood, seen through the fact of non-duality. And this training can only be carried out through co-operation between a pupil and one who has the priceless knowledge to pass on, through a partnership which must be observed and maintained if the training is to be successful.

Just as you must learn to tune in your radio before you can make a contact with the music which forever permeates the atmosphere, so you must learn to tune in your psychological instrument before you can become aware of the subtle music of the spirit which interpenetrates you and all else. The preliminary training in this manipulation of the psychological recording machine is given through traditional practices grouped under the one heading of mind control -

which is more appropriately called 'mind direction'.

Mind direction - yes, but in what direction? It is true that the teachings of the Vedanta and the law of dharma postulate a final fact, a unity, pure Consciousness. But this is a world-shaking doctrine, one which, if fully understood and subscribed to, can make man God and the world a shadow of reality. How is our man to direct his mind towards something so vast that he cannot fathom or accept it at present? Here the great Teachers of the Yoga have provided two truth diviners - more potent and unerring than any water diviner. They will assist the student in this practice of mind control, mind expansion and mind direction, and all pupils are traditionally expected to make full use of them during their training.

These two truth diviners or diviners of hidden spiritual treasure, are called in Sanskrit vichara and viveka - enquiry and discrimination. Vichara or enquiry takes precedence during the preliminary training. It involves an enquiry into the validity of this claim of non-duality. It must be conducted through a study of the acknowledged classics and the words of a traditional Teacher, or of those who have been trained by him. At this stage the acceptance of the truth of non-duality by the would-be disciple must necessarily be theoretical, accepted as a premise to make investigation possible - but it will have to be substantiated or repudiated in due course.

You may have noticed that if you accept any premise, things at first have a convenient way of grouping themselves in support of it. The only way you will know whether the premise has truth in it or not is to watch how long the supporting facts can uphold the theory put forward. In order to judge this, the second truth diviner is brought into play. *Viveka*, discrimination, is that glorious attribute of unprejudiced scrutiny which is the vehicle of lovers of truth - not of the lovers of the marvellous or of wishful thinking. The grandeur of this system of thought - Advaita Vedanta - is demonstrated by the precedence it gives at the outset to two such impersonal qualities as *vichara* and *viveka*, and its students are expected at first to rely on them completely.

Now discrimination, *viveka*, can be carried on at all levels of consciousness. It is a characteristic of the higher reaches of the mind and not only of its logical strata, although in the higher reaches it works with lightning speed and illumined power and certainty, and it is then known as spiritual intuition. *Viveka* will make use of ancient traditions and it will also turn to the findings of modern science. It will bring the pupil face to face with statements which were made with complete assurance by the Teachers of old, and which he will now recognise again in modern dress. It will direct him to science, and under the promptings of enquiry and discrimination, he will discover there many things which will assist him in breaking away from the mental world he used to believe to be so real.

For instance, he will find that whatever his mind becomes conscious of, is in fact a substitute for the original stimulus which gave shape to that conception. This substitute comes down through the channels of his senses and his memory, transformed by that mind for his edification or his misery, but for nothing more lasting than that. *Maya*, unreality, the dream world - these words will not seem to be quite so extravagant when enquiry and discrimination have started to test the ground.

It is under the direction of enquiry and discrimination that the pupil begins to become aware of the aimless activity which has for so long been taking place within his mind. He realises, through enquiry, that he can lessen and direct this activity. He is now introduced to mind control *par excellence*. He begins to grasp its purpose, and to allow that purpose to govern the practice.

So long as mind control is looked upon as of paramount importance, carried out as a forcible regulation of the mental activities in order to establish mastery over them, that practice will remain a dry empirical one. But if through patient enquiry the fact is grasped that the higher powers and subtle reactions will never enter a full, preoccupied and noisy mind, the processes which aim at emptying and transfiguring the mind will be seen to have meaning and creative power, and the pupil will grow as he attempts them.

It is not possible to say how long each stage in the training will take before it begins to fructify, for each pupil differs in his understanding of their value and purpose. These growing and successive impacts of enquiry, discrimination and the consequent longing for growth or liberation, slightly resemble spiritual or psychological meals. When a man is hungry he eats with interest and then is satisfied, because he is busy digesting what he has received. But there comes a time when he will inevitably feel hungry again and will begin to look for another meal. If the pupil will only believe that this is the natural procedure in his case also, he will learn that speed is less important than absorption and acceptance of the teachings already given. If he will wait until his digestion has done its work and he again feels the impulse to take nourishment, he will get

the full value of what he already has and what he is
about to receive. He will grow in stature and without
distortion.

It is the feeling of need, the outcome of patient
digestion, which gives results, and not the conventional
following out of a pattern of training. The Teachers of
old fully realised this, and they prepared fresh meals for
their pupils only at psychological and not at regular
intervals.

For instance, up to a certain point the pupil has been
reading, discussing with others, if he is fortunate
enough to find anyone interested, and communing with
himself on his findings. If he does this patiently and
without hurry, he will probably now become even more
aware of his mental processes and reactions, and the
want of discipline which still exists within his mind. He
will begin to feel a hunger for some more potent food
which will produce a deeper and stronger concentration
in him.

He has probably heard by now, and is beginning to
hope, that logic, discrimination and mental dissection
are not his highest powers, and that his highest power
has not yet appeared on his mental horizon. This is the
intuitional power, the inspirational and transcendent
faculty, which does not work through any medium, but
yet gives direct knowledge to its possessor in the form
of unquestioning certainty. Until the mind has been
brought - not to a standstill - but until it has produced
sufficient faith and understanding to cause it to regulate
its pace and direct its activities inward, instead of
glissading over the surface of many subjects - until the
mind has done this, the intuitive sense will not emerge
from within it.

Once the pupil knows that this power, though not his

as yet, is his by right, he will be fortified. He will turn instinctively and perhaps even hopefully to the practice of meditation and contemplation; for up to now his essays in both these practices have probably been efforts to learn how to apply his mind and will.

The whole progress of the learner has been from extreme and instinctive mental activity (generally of an extrovertive nature), to an inner, conscious and directed stillness, which bears little resemblance to the early restless preoccupations of the untrained mind. This progress from mental noise to silence, from repletion to emptiness, is the way in which the expectant mind prepares itself for the coming of the spiritual truth. This talk is an attempt to indicate the essential aspects of the mode of progression of a traditional pupil, and the nature of this preparation is, without a doubt, the first essential to be grasped.

According to the spiritual classics, there are two types of minds into which the spiritual truth will not enter. In the *Katha Upanishad* it is said: 'No-one whose senses are not under control and whose mind is not collected and at rest, can acquire this knowledge', and I have tried to give some reasons for this. The other mind which cannot as yet receive the spiritual truth, is held to be one which still has the capacity to sting, and consciously exercises it. Here again it is said that before receiving the truth in its fullness, the aspirant must have relinquished the power to wound anyone by thought, word or deed.

You will now see why the moment when the learner first detected the workings of the law of *dharma* in his life and actions was such an important one for him. The Teachers of this Yoga will not recognise a pupil to be an established yogi until he has ceased to live in the three stages of the training and is manifesting their results in his daily life. This means that he must have had experience of these stages and have passed through them. First, there was the outward-turning, active, egoistic stage, when, as we have seen, he was for ever experimenting and striving. It was followed by the inner stage when the pupil became the withdrawn enjoyer and meditator, expanding his consciousness and nourishing himself on the inner spiritual truth. The final stage brings the development of the capacity within himself not only to seek and to enjoy, but to manifest and pass on to others what he has received and discovered.

If it is not too far-fetched and wanting in reverence, we could say that during his training a pupil successfully assumes the roles of those great actors in the Bible story of Martha, Mary and the Lord. As Martha he has polished and cleansed the *antahkarana*, and has anxiously busied himself with questions of inner and outer nourishment, comfort and worldly toil. As Mary he has located and drawn near, in stillness and attention, to the source from where the true food and wisdom will come. As the Lord he has reached the stage where the source of all activity, stillness, nourishment and bliss is known to be within his own Self, from where he can pass it on to all who will receive it. The transition from the Martha to the Mary stage is made by ceasing to be earthily active and responsible, and becoming inwardly quiescent and yet awake and receptive. It is a transition worthy to be made, for a few moments' work done with the fervour of Mary are worth hours of patient polishing by Martha.

By now some may be feeling that one of the first essentials in the spiritual awakening of man has been forgotten. The details of his training and the ingredients for his meal have been set out very carefully, but there is no fire to warm him or to cook with. Worship and devotion - where are they? Surely only they can light the fire which will produce life-giving food?

Worship is said to be an inner movement of the heart, born of growing recognition, and it will not come into being until the object of devotion and worship has been partially revealed. In the usual course, the philosophy of non-duality does not deal with objects. But the beauty of the supreme truth, omnipresent as it is, can be detected and worshipped through any focus consecrated for the purpose. Shri Rama, Shri Krishna, Jesus, the Teacher, and even less obvious focuses than these, can be regarded as visible vehicles for the revelation and contemplation of that beauty. All action, all effort, is in fact directed towards this end alone, namely to recognise and become identified with the supreme truth and to communicate a ray of its glory to the world.

There are methods of increasing the power of worship and devotion, but they must all lead to the goal of identification. The deep meditation, the repetition of the name of God, the dedicated daily life, are all practices for one end only: that through purification, a man may draw nearer and nearer to that centre which is both the centre of all perfection and of his own being, and in the end be merged in it for ever. This is an aspect of the teaching which cannot be described or exhibited to one who is merely considering entering Yoga. It must be directly experienced and practised by him in the way which best suits his own nature.

XII

THE INNER TRANSFORMATION

IN THE ANCIENT classic called *The Conference of the Birds* by Farid ud-Din Attar, the Persian poet and philosopher, there is a verse which says:

> God is all, and things have only a nominal value;
> The world visible and the world invisible are
>   only Himself;
> There is none but Him.

Attar is showing by these words that this all-pervading, pure and changeless spirit lies above, below and within all phenomena, and that a direct realisation of it must be the goal and climax of all life, for man will never know himself and be at peace until he knows this spirit directly. All earthly and subtle wonders emanate from it, for it is the matrix from which all springs forth. Man is the most astonishing wonder of all these wonders and he exists in their midst, biding the time when each in turn will give up its secrets under his adventurous investigation. For he has a divine thirst within him, a determination, subconscious yet driving, to know the truth, not only about himself, but also about all that surrounds him.

If we look back on his climb towards knowledge, we shall see that when he started his career as a conscious though primitive being, man was like a child at a fair, fascinated, frightened by what he saw, greedy for more, yet taken in by all the tricks of the trade. He was surrounded by a world of matter, subtle and gross, which, as we know, is held by the Vedanta philosophy to be governed by a divine law or intention, but which, to him then, must have been a spectacle either of terror or of opportunity. The laws of time and space, attraction and repulsion, gravity and so forth, which operate around us, are surely the pledge of the presence of an all-pervading Power, but while man was in his spiritual and mental infancy, they manifested un-noticed or rather misunderstood by him.

In this primitive state, he was not aware of the fact that he was the only conscious spectator of this scene of wonder. Animals, fish and birds exist within it, but unconsciously, that is to say instinctively, while obeying its laws in many cases better than man does. But man alone is actively conscious of multiplicity - the matter and variety which surrounds him - and he watched it through his as yet unknown mind, which, according to Vedanta, is itself composed of subtle matter and yet which records the various manifestations of matter which exist around it.

At this early stage, man invested whatever he saw or experienced with a life similar to his own. To him, his mental states were induced by living invisible forces. Hatred, revenge and the sense of power, were indications of the presence and action of powerful beings. And so were the outer storms also - floods, pestilence, eclipses, earthquakes and the like; to him everything was alive and full of mystery. The only thing which as yet he did not consider to be full of mystery, was the greatest mystery of all: his own mind. That mind was still unaware of itself, being solely engaged with outer objects and with recording and assessing them. This means that man had not yet learnt to look on his mind as an object, and to watch its activities and assess them.

As we have said, according to the teaching of the Vedanta, the mind is composed of subtle yet inert matter. Its characteristic of constant change both in movement, quality and intensity, is superimposed on it by the supreme principle which interpenetrates it. This inner organ, or *antahkarana* as it is called in Sanskrit, operates on two levels. Firstly there is the lower mind or *manas*, which is the recording, receiving centre, and the seat of the outward-going activities. The other level of operation is that of the higher mind or *buddhi*, which is the diagnosing and discriminating centre.

The lower or outward-going centre, or the *manas*, may be said to perform the functions of an usherette in the great theatre of the mind. It contacts and without selection directs that which it encounters, into the presence of the *buddhi*, the discriminating power. A writer has said that its action is like that of a gate, for it indiscriminately lets through sensations one by one into the higher regions of the *buddhi*. It summons all man's personal qualities and instincts to assist it in the work - the ego with its prejudices and preferences, the memory and the emotions are among these. They reach the *buddhi* and while it is still untrained, colour its findings, weaving a web of distortion around unfortunate vulnerable man.

The higher centre of activity, the *buddhi*, also acts on two levels. The lower *buddhi* diagnoses and discriminates, while the higher receives and responds to very subtle impulses and impressions only. Discrimination and recognition through inference and logic is the function of the lower *buddhi*, while the higher *buddhi* is the field of the great powers of immediate perception, inspiration and intuition. The difference in the quality of activity in the lower and higher mind is due to a difference in their power of reception, which means in their perception of the divine light, or knowledge, which, though permeating them both, is unequally recorded by them.

Roughly speaking, all yogic exercises and practices are designed to produce a balance, harmony and quietude in the mind as a whole. This will enable the inspirational and intuitional powers of the higher buddhi to manifest and direct the general mental activity, that is, to direct the lower as well as the higher mind. The practices of mind control, dispassion, and above all the slow entry into the realm of meditation, are to be engaged in intelligently, and not in a ferociously ascetic spirit. These practices, when working together, will produce in the whole mind first a balance and then a vacuum. This does not mean an emptiness, but a state which is not identified with the diverse impacts to which it is subject, and is not unsettled by them. It is in this mental calm, the hallmark of the presence of the powers of the higher buddhi, that the final wonders and transformations of the Yoga take place.

But when we left our man in order to say a few things about his mental instrument, he was still in his primitive state. His mental life was still confined to his lower recording mind, which is under the direct influence of the instincts and emotions and the unevolved ego. The words 'unevolved ego' have no doubt a strange sound to some. One gets the impression, during the preliminary period of investigation and study, that maybe we shall have to lose this ego, or kill it, or somehow put it out of action. But the teaching of the Vedanta is that the ego is basically divine, that it is potentially the 'I' of man, and that in the two centres, the higher *buddhi* and the ego, is hidden the secret of immortality and the key of release.

As the higher *buddhi*, the apex of the mind, begins to bring its great powers of inner direct vision and intuition into operation, the ego detaches itself from the lower pandemonium. It rises and sees its true nature mirrored in that clear and reflecting light, which now fills the highest region of the mind; and once these two, the ego and the higher *buddhi*, know their common origin, the play will be over and man will be free, for he will know who he in fact is.

Rejection of the world and its joys does not make this consummation a certainty. Renunciation and asceticism may be undertaken as lip service, without any real understanding of the Truth as it is taught in the philosophy. Release will come through the discovery by the ego of its true nature, when seen through the mediumship of the now dominating and shining higher *buddhi*.

Now at some point in time man's first transformation took place and he took his first steps towards a recognition of the existence of his mind, and therefore the possibility of the existence of that transcendent state which has just been hinted at. This recognition must have developed very slowly, but he must at last have become aware of the importance to him of his own mind, and have gained at least an inkling of the powers and riches hidden within it.

What brought about this interior change, when it did come? Why was man not satisfied to be an eternal spectator of the play? It would have been an exciting and rewarding enough role surely. You will remember that Attar says: 'Things have only a nominal value' - meaning a changing value, an unsubstantial changing value. It is this that causes the significance of objects and happenings to change as man's understanding of their nature rises and changes. For man also, in common with all other objects, himself changes, and he changes in proportion as he yields to the growing domination of the light within him.

Why should that light increase at all, for it is already divine, which is another name for 'full'? Why does it not remain for ever giving forth the same intensity of illumination, as does a candle or a torch? The growth, the expansion takes place not within the light itself but within the object in which the light is revealed. This light is fullness, being, the true life of all. It does not increase or grow, but like a divine solvent it causes changes to take place in phenomena. Man will always be restless until this transmutation has taken place within him and he directly experiences the reality, which is his own being, without barriers of any kind. Until that moment comes, as the Elizabethan poet Marlowe has said, man is:

> Still climbing after knowledge infinite,
> And always moving as the restless spheres.

No fitting word has ever been discovered for this fullness. Sometimes it is called Truth or Reality, sometimes God, sometimes Life of life, sometimes Bliss, but no word gives any indication of what it in fact is. It will only be known at the moment of the final transformation. At present we apprehend it through its effects, and more important, through the testimony of those who have had its direct experience.

Well, granted that at a certain point man becomes aware of the slow approach of a sunrise, how does that new and higher territory of his mind make itself known to him under this growing revelation of light? In the *Katha Upanishad* it says: 'The Creator made man's senses outgoing. A wise man turned within, and he beheld the Self, face to face.' These wise men are the vanguards of humanity, men whose mental admixture makes it possible for them to go ahead of their brothers and anticipate the path they must follow. These leaders, intuitive and dedicated, are not only to be found among men. One can perceive the potential emergence of their qualities in the kingdom of the animals and birds also. You see selfish animals, quarrelsome egoistic birds, nervous placating animals, but there are also noble, self-sacrificing creatures, who set a standard for their kind, and for man also, and it is they who emerge as the leaders of others.

The leaders of men - the gurus and *rishis* (seers) - through their inspired spiritual and mental understanding, were the first to penetrate into the unworked mine of the *antahkarana*. They opened it up with all its treasures for the good of their fellow men. These spiritual pioneers lived aeons ago, and their descendants live today. The Vedas and the Upanishads and probably many other spiritual classics in other parts of the world, are many of them thousands of years old. The *Bhagavad Gita* is itself a part of the *Mahabharata*, one of the most ancient records, and it is still called the 'Bible of India'. The Buddhist and the Christian teachings are also raised upon foundations which are far more ancient than they are themselves.

Man's spiritual and mental awareness began to develop from the time when the Truth was given forth by these spiritual teachers by word of mouth. The teachings we possess today were cherished and passed on orally by them for hundreds, perhaps thousands of years before they were written down.

We have said that the first transformation in man was probably brought about by obscure yet directed searching. It was due to this spiritual direction and to the fact that his mind, although he was unaware of it, was inevitably expanding in light, that man became conscious of the qualities residing in this inner tool, this instrument of precision with which he would be able to discover the secrets of the objects surrounding him. Thus began his search for the ultimate truth. The search has been proceeding on two parallel lines ever since. There are, on the one hand, those who employ their powers of deduction, logic and discrimination - the assets of the lower buddhi. And there are others who use the inner and supra-mental powers of inspiration, direct vision and intuition. These are the tools of the higher buddhi.

Those who are still ruled by manas, the instinctive, emotional lower mind, cannot be said to follow a path as yet. Their mental and spiritual life is still only at its beginning. The first defined path is the way of the lower buddhi. It attracts the scientist, the inventor, and those who quarry out truth through experiment, deduction and logical thinking. But their findings have been obtained through the workings of a finite instrument and they will also be finite, that is, liable to change.

The second path is walked by those who have prepared and directed their minds under spiritual guidance. They act and make their discoveries impelled by those supra-mental powers which operate in this region and which have direct cognition and realisation as their fruit. Slowly the inevitable fact of an all-pervading essence - One-without-a-second - must have been intuited by these adventurous explorers. Fortunate they were, and are, for this recognition causes the ego to lose its individual contour and thus brings about the final transformation, which is the natural and spontaneous acceptance of non-duality.

Let us now try to relate this general account of man's inner progress to our individual cases. Everybody starts his babyhood as a primitive being, reacting, recording, with his senses ever outward-going, his instincts manifesting with his first breath - that is to say, with his lower mind in nominal control. The slow recognition of his own individual existence, the emergence of his ego, follows inevitably. Then he will be, not free to choose - things are not as simple as that - but he will feel drawn, however unconsciously, to one of these two paths, either towards empirical knowledge - the path of the lower *buddhi* - or towards the path of the higher *buddhi*. Once he has begun, he may persevere on that path to the end, or he may, and he often does, change on the way.

It is held traditionally that there are two qualities which are essential to the spiritual aspirant on both paths. The first is *vichara*, or enquiry, and the other is reverence. For out of these two mental attitudes - which are in fact spiritual - will appear, in due course, knowledge, devotion and the selfless sharing of the Truth with others.

Enquiry is that investigation, patient, unprejudiced and attentive, which can only be undertaken by a true explorer, never by an amasser of facts. This enquiry opens up the way to knowledge. Reverence will inevitably be called forth from a true pupil as he proceeds and the vision of the expanse and grandeur of the knowledge he is pursuing breaks upon him. These two qualities are essential for the walkers on either path, and both use them. The scientific investigators, the inventors, doctors, geologists and many others, all those in fact who deduce and diagnose and apparently obtain their findings as a result of mental activity, show that they possess insatiable *vichara*, and they reverence their material as well.

The yogic training for the mastery of the mind, for meditation and finally for transcendence, resembles the technique of an accomplished mountaineer, and the mind may be visualised as a great mountain. The spiritual journey, or rather the spiritual training, is a climb up the mind. The disciple under the direction of his Teacher passes through its different altitudes until he arrives at the summit of the mind. Like the crest of a mountain, this summit is surrounded by the winds of heaven and the winds of inspiration, and is not shut in by any object.

The lower reaches of the outgoing, busy, lower mind are like the foothills at the base of a great mountain. Here there is luxurious vegetation and animal life, although very little direct sunlight. There is also plenty of diversion and temptation in the shape of the inhabitants of the district, who are always ready to waste the time of the mountaineer and dissipate his energy in talk and general curiosity. This, I understand, is the invariable experience of climbers in both fields at this stage.

When the climber has at last prepared himself physically and mentally and has decided on what he will discard and what he will take with him, which is settled by the preliminary training, he sets off on his way. Very soon vegetable and animal life begins to disappear and the landscape becomes bare, yet it has a beauty of its own. Now his powers of discrimination and decision are constantly being brought into play as he wins foothold after foothold up the side. He is learning also how to harbour his energy in order to meet the many demands which may be made on it as he ascends. In other words, the plane of the lower *buddhi* has been reached, and it may take the pupil a long time to climb beyond it. When he does at last arrive beyond the snow line, many experiences come to the climber on both the inner and the outer mountain, which are known traditionally but about which few can speak.

To attain the summit of a mountain, or to rise through the mind to its apex, calls for the perfecting of certain qualities. We have mentioned them already. These qualities are a sense of direction, the practice of unprejudiced enquiry into the nature and scope of the enterprise, reverence arising from a recognition of its nature, and finally dedication of the resources, inner and outer, of both mountaineer and disciple to the quest they have undertaken.

But similes should not be stretched too far, otherwise they snap like elastic and sting. The progression up the mind is of course not as neat and obvious as I have made it out to be. Everyone has his own particular level at which he feels more secure than he does at any other. For some it is the level of the lower mind and for others either the lower or the higher *buddhi*. Some remain at the same level all their life long, others are restless to be up and away. But at some point in some incarnation, every man must start to climb his mountain. He may often turn back, but once the desire for freedom has awakened in him, he will at last move on and ultimately reach the summit. The only level from which no-one will ever descend is the crest of the mind.

During the ascent every exterior and interior situation is capable of maturing the technique of the disciple, just as the various problems of the ascent increase the experience of the mountaineer. Every emotion, every happening, every experience, has a teaching value in both schools of training and is used for furthering the final purpose. The great yogi, Swami Rama Tirtha, says:

Vice and virtue, joy and sorrow
Were the rungs of the ladder to the chamber
    of the Friend.
You may burn this ladder now,
I shall come down no more.

Enquiry or *vichara* can always be practised by anyone, starting at any time, but it should be given a definite form. A definite time of the day should be allotted to it, and a definite amount of time also. It is wise to seek advice about which classics you should choose for study at first. The following meditation, which is an ancient prayer from the Upanishads, will strengthen your sense of direction:

OM. From the unreal lead me to the real,
    From darkness to light,
    From death to immortality. OM.

This meditation can be performed in the morning or in the evening, or both, and it is helpful to bring it before the mind during the day. Keep relaxed and reflect on its meaning as often as you can. Above all, speaking from personal experience, do not quarrel with the mind if it is unable to accept the meaning of the meditation or to concentrate on it straight away.

There is a verse from a Sanskrit classic which says:

His form is not an object of vision,
No-one beholds Him with the eyes,
But they who through reflection realise Him
Through the pure buddhi, they become immortal.

XIII

THE FINAL TEACHINGS

THE PURPOSE of Yoga is the bringing of a pupil to the knowledge of God, or *Brahman*. The final stage in spiritual unfoldment is reached partly by a preoccupation with the mastery of the mind, which means learning to eliminate a great deal of rubbish from it; partly by the purification of the mind, which involves the substitution of a few great concepts for the endless detail it usually contains; and partly by carrying out traditional practices for the control of its energy and its direction. This direction has become clearer as the pupil's grasp on the philosophy and the yogic psychology has grown firmer. Nevertheless, his mind still remains a mind, that is to say, it still acts as an assessor, working only under stimulus, an instrument of increasingly accurate precision maybe, but always with limited capacity and endurance.

According to the yogic psychology, the mind or inner organ or centre of reaction and perception, is merely an instrument or medium for the manifestation of Consciousness. It is neither Consciousness itself, nor is it conscious in its own right, any more than a radio is musical, or music in the abstract. The mind manifests Consciousness, but it also limits it by virtue of its heterogeneous nature.

The pupil is now entering a stage about which very little can be said or proved, and where one must provisionally accept the testimony of those enlightened sages who have had immediate experience of this

139

condition. These seers affirm that basically man is immortal spirit, and that therefore fundamentally he must also be pure and partless, because only the immaculate is beyond change, and therefore immortal. Like a mass of matter which, when examined by the microscope or other scientific implements, reveals itself to be without density, all light, movement and energy, so when man is correctly known he is found to be neither body nor mind, nor psychological reactions and restrictions, but spirit - Being alone. He is seen to be limitless Consciousness, self-luminous and blissful. This vision, when achieved, is the goal of human life, for it leads into the final unbroken, yet normal state, known as the 'seedless', the nirvikalpa samadhi. It is called seedless because it is productive of nothing further, being the supreme end in itself.

To express such words or even to believe them theoretically will not bring release to distracted, questioning humanity. Man must have direct personal experience of their truth. Nothing else will do for him, and until he achieves this he will either reserve judgement, while giving the statement a sympathetic hearing, or he will shrug his shoulders, and saying: 'What some people can make themselves believe!' will go his ways.

But is there in fact such a supreme and final state and are there traditional methods through which the pupil may know it? The practices by which the mind can be made increasingly sensitive, pure and finally luminous, have been known and practised since the earliest days. Speaking generally, there is first the intelligent exercise of vichara or enquiry. This involves an enquiry not only into the philosophy but into its inner implications and the significance of the training. Then come the practices which are aided by this *vichara* and are framed to gain mastery over the inner agitation and impulses both mental and emotional. Lastly there is the conscious awakening of reverence and worship for the supreme spirit, all-pervading and all light, and also for the majestic universe of men, beasts and objects, with the cosmic laws which guide it.

It is through these traditional practices and his living desire for knowledge that the pupil learns how to transcend his recognised mental powers and bring other faculties into use. These little known sensitive faculties are extensions, so to say, of the discriminative reason which is lodged in his *buddhi*, or higher mind. Such powers will not reveal their hidden presence until the ego-direction of the mind, which manifests as prejudices and preferences, has been broken down and the limited nature of the lower mind is recognised and therefore no longer relied upon.

These instruments or powers do not operate through reason and inference. They act under the direct light of Consciousness and not through any medium. They produce instantaneous results, such as immediate and faultless penetration, an intuitive recognition, not of concepts or facts but of their inner significance and quality, and also a recognition of the possibility of abstract states of consciousness. They are awakened by deep meditation.

Our Teacher has said that *Brahman* or God is recognised (and his use of this word is significant) through the practice of meditation. But true meditation can never take place while there is noise and ferment in the mind, caused by the devices of the ego and a belief that the acquisition of power and empirical knowledge will bring permanent satisfaction and must therefore be acquired at all costs. This fact indicates that ego-display is an unsurmountable barrier to inner expansion.

The seeming criticism of empirical knowledge is not meant to imply that this Yoga denies its importance. Adhyatma Yoga is in fact a synthesis of knowledge, identification and trained action. The acquisition of knowledge is a supremely purifying activity. It would be as impossible to deny its function and value in both the empirical and the spiritual life as it would be to deny that the moon gives light as well as the sun. Nevertheless the moon will always be a reflection and when the sun is up, she will abdicate in his favour and become a disc in the sky.

The disciple will never obtain information in the ordinary sense of the word through the agency of these higher powers, nor will he experience a variety of reactions. But through their instrumentality he will become aware of, and embrace, the living spirit which animates all the objects of *sansara* (the world). In due time, through the use of these powers, he will obtain an inner sight of the supreme Power which surrounds and interpenetrates both himself and the whole cosmos. This will make him feel as a God, or rather it will revive his long-forgotten memory of his real nature - namely that he is and always has been the one spirit, the all-pervasive reality or Truth, immortal and, we are assured, blissful.

The mind is by nature finite and heterogeneous and will only be able to provide its owner with finite and temporal data. But according to the Teachers of Yoga, a condition does exist - supra-mental and final - where the relationship between subject and object is perforce abandoned. This condition will be spontaneously recognised and remembered when it swims into view, and when fully revealed it will envelop the whole scene and also the one who experiences it.

And what again are those higher powers which bring about this higher mental state? The capacity for egoless absorption, intuition and inspiration. These are the powers, but they are not the final condition itself. They merely reveal it, and they are rendered active by the higher teachings and training of the Yoga - principally by deep meditation and contemplation.

No-one wishes to learn interminably - the preparations for a journey cannot go on for ever. Every pupil who is worthy of the name works so that he may at last be able to put the Truth which stands behind the Advaita philosophy into practice, first verifying it and then incorporating it into himself through direct realisation. Our task is to indicate how he crosses the bridge between discipleship and adepthood, and reaches unbroken and complete freedom at last.

The mind is both the cause of man's bondage and the means of his release. To use a simile: the rays of light, visible and invisible, and their action when in contact with the earth, will always be impeded and checkered by objects, obstructions and the moving atmospheric conditions. The primal source from which the light springs cannot be affected; nevertheless its manifestation is hampered. But the light shines unhindered and ever more fully revealed in the distant and empty strata of the atmosphere. In the same way, the empirical mind, forever in contact with the multiplicity of maya, allows only a fitful display of consciousness to be revealed while in that condition. But in its higher states where quiet and harmony reign, this consciousness will shine unimpeded and self-luminous, pervading all.

Now, as the still limited and ego-directed intelligence, made lighter by the training, slowly rises in this clearing mental atmosphere, it begins to experience a condition of illumined and blissful awareness. Although still conscious of its psychological fetters, it also experiences the pull of gravitation towards the divine spirit which, like a magnet, is continuously drawing all creation towards itself. The psychological restraints, both voluntary and sub-conscious, which have been actuated in the past by reason or psychological biases, are beginning to loosen. Now comes the time when the depth and quality of the pupil's understanding of the motives underlying the training will be revealed. For unless he has grasped the inner implications of the teachings, as well as the philosophical and practical facts, he may indeed experience a growing sense of freedom, but he will remain suspended between earth and heaven until he has become more fully identified with the Truth he seeks.

The Teachers say that the acid test of rooted knowledge is spontaneous reaction, not the studied and reasoned carrying out of the spiritual laws, however correct and edifying such performances may appear to be. Therefore at this stage each pupil experiences and manifests the result of his own understanding of the Truth. For instance, the practice of the higher meditation is traditionally held to produce, at some time, the two samadhis - samadhi meaning a supramental state of consciousness. The lower samadhi is called the samadhi with seed or results, and is a passing condition. The higher, the nirvikalpa or seedless samadhi, when once had, is never lost and is productive of no results. It is the end in itself.

The lower *samadhi* is indeed a state of sustained concentration where there is absorption in the subject of the meditation. In an egoless and pure mind, this may be productive of great bliss and enlightenment. But on the other hand, as our Teacher used to tell us, where the significance of the training is not grasped or accepted, those who practise this *samadhi* may still emerge from it as spiritual bankrupts.

He used to tell the story of a fakir who through long and devoted practice had mastered the art of concentration, culminating in the lower *samadhi*. He was poor, and to the outward view, an ascetic. But he ardently and secretly desired to be recognised as a man of spiritual power, and also as the possessor of patrons. In order to stand well with the people, he longed for a horse on which he could ride and make a good impression. One day, the Maharajah of a neighbouring state, hearing of his powers, said he would like to witness them. The man was summoned, and after assuming the correct posture and intoning many mantrams, he did go into meditation and passed into the lower *samadhi*. For a long time he sat withdrawn and statue-like before the reverent and impressed Maharajah. Then at last he opened his eyes and all the Court leaned forward to hear the first holy words to issue from his lips. 'Maharajah', he said, 'give me a horse. I want a horse, your Highness.'

This is only a tale, told, I suspect, by our Teacher to make us realise that the possession of powers, even such powers as the power of absorption in meditation, does not necessarily imply the possession of spiritual power, although of course this may be there in its fullness. But the higher *samadhi* is productive of no outward result and is the direct experience of reality. It is inviolate, without end, and can never be tampered with, for it cannot be had until the final identification is achieved.

These states and the methods which bring them about have been dealt with in the *Bhagavad Gita*. This classic contains the most explicit and traditional information on spiritual instruction that has come down to us from the past. In the *Gita*, a Teacher passes his pupil through the whole gamut of the training, and the reactions of this pupil have been commented on by the great philosopher and Guru, Shri Shankaracharya. We see the Teacher wean his pupil from a reliance on his reasoning mind and then from reliance on its higher powers; and finally we see him awaken in his pupil a complete reliance on and recognition of himself as the supreme spirit.

During the narrative the disciple makes four ejaculations, which come at four crises in his spiritual unfoldment, and they may serve to clarify the points just made. The first is the ejaculation which must be made by every man who seriously seeks spiritual knowledge. Here the pupil, Prince Arjuna cries:

> My mind is in confusion, I am bewildered as to what is my duty, I beseech Thee to teach me what to do.

At this moment Arjuna is at a standstill - mental, moral and spiritual. He thinks that although his own mind may not be clear and reasoned enough to guide him, the mind of a Teacher must be so - for he is used to relying on his mind and physical strength alone. The Teacher, Shri Krishna, who is in fact an Incarnation of God manifesting in the role of a Guru, accepts him

forthwith - that is, he takes him to himself and begins
to instruct him.

Having first granted Arjuna a flash of the highest
Truth about his real nature, in order, we imagine, to
arrest his attention, he gives him his first psychological
lesson. Incidentally, the information Shri Krishna
imparts at this juncture is repeated from time to time
throughout the *Gita*, even to its very culmination. It is
that no outer problem can ever be solved without the
presence of inner rectitude and a conscious recognition
of the universal spirit and the law of *dharma* or
righteousness. In other words, he introduces his
disciple not to an inner and high solution of his
problem, but to those character-forming virtues which
will pacify and purify his mind and decentralise his ego;
and only after doing this does he impart the specific
discipline and higher psychological training. For five
chapters he shines the light of Truth on his pupil's mind
from every angle, and at last, in the sixth chapter, he
opens his instructions on meditation.

We can imagine that as a result of this Prince Arjuna
is becoming dimly aware of an inner world of higher
power and values and also of the quality and vital being
or Consciousness interpenetrating both his Teacher,
himself and all the objects around him. In other words,
he is beginning to sense an expansion within himself.
Consequently, a great desire arises in his mind for the
powers of higher perception which will enable him to
see and know that which hitherto has been unseen and
unknown by him. And therefore he makes his second
ejaculation. Now he no longer cries: 'My mind is
confused, my senses are deluded', though in fact they
still are - but he cries:

My delusion has gone! I have heard (that is, through the slowly concentrating mind and senses), I have heard from Thee of Thine inexhaustible greatness! O Lord, show me that omniscient form of Thine, that I may know Thee.

Once again he has reached a halting place. But now he is becoming aware of unseen forces and also of his own powers and of a wish to absorb himself in their contemplation. So the Teacher, the Lord Incarnate, who knows well the true condition of his disciple, centres his concentration and reveals to him an inner vision - unbelievable, unsupportable to the senses - of multiplicity in its relation to unity. The sight robs Arjuna of his courage and fills his still unpurified mind with terror, and, what is more revealing, with a conviction of his utter weakness and insignificance. Without stretching the point too far, it might be said that Arjuna is now in a state resembling the temporary and lower *samadhi* with seed. But he is unable to support it, owing to the still agitated state of his senses and the insufficiency of his knowledge. His mind is disintegrating and he now makes his third ejaculation which comes in the form of a desperate cry:

O Lord, my mind is distracted with terror. Withdraw Thine awful form. Have mercy on me and manifest before me again thine embodied form, I beseech Thee!

Thereupon, like a flash, the vision ends. The Teacher Shri Krishna resumes his familiar human form, and his disciple, Arjuna, the strain of his concentration lessening and his terror gone, emerges from that blinding flash of awareness and makes his last ejaculation:

> O Lord, I am serene again, I have returned to my normal condition.

But again he errs. He has not reached the normal condition, which is beyond reaction and desire. He has still to address his Teacher again, and when he does so it will not be to beseech him for this or for that, but to state a fact to him - a fact which will end the training for ever and show him to be free.

At present the pupil is still in the transitional state, between earth and heaven, and not able to enter fully into either. This is due to his psychological limitations, which are still unresolved, and also to his still narrow understanding of the significance of the truths he has received. When he has become finally settled in his true nature, he will effortlessly absorb all into his limitless being, and he will at last enter the seedless, the endless *samadhi*.

So once more, and for the last time, the Teacher takes up his instruction. This time he reveals the highest and most purifying aspects of the philosophy, those spiritual facts which stand round and support the supreme Truth. But he still interpenetrates them with reminders of the necessity for righteous conduct, egolessness and quietude. He still gives the injunction that the knowledge which is now being imparted must later be carried into practice in empirical life. This must take the form of service and that love of man which springs from a recognition of the brotherhood and basic unity of all.

Slowly the teachings come to an end, like the close of

a great musical work. Now the disciple makes a simple statement, not an ejaculation. He says:

> My ignorance has gone. By Thy grace I have regained the memory of my true state.

That is all, and this time he is right, for there is no outer demonstration, no strain, no contact to be maintained with anything. He is safe, he is fearless and free, immersed in that *nirvikalpa samadhi* which is without end and the outcome of the direct experience of reality. He has regained that glory which was his before the worlds began.

GLOSSARY

Adhyatma   the supreme Self.

Adhyatma Yoga the Yoga of Self-Knowledge; the spiritual science concerned with the real nature of man.

Advaita   non-duality; the philosophy of Advaita holds that *Brahman* alone exists without a second.

Ahankara   the ego; the 'I' taken as doer and experiencer.

Ananda   bliss.

Antahkarana   the mind or 'inner organ' of the individual; the thinking and feeling principle in the human personality.

Atman   the higher Self of man, which is identical with the supreme reality, *Brahman*

Avatara   an Incarnation of the Lord; a direct descent of God to earth in a physical body.

Bhagavad Gita the 'Song of the Lord' - a spiritual classic in which the *Avatara* Lord Krishna summarises the teachings of Yoga for his disciple Arjuna.

Brahman   the absolute reality; the highest Godhead beyond attributes.

151

Buddhi	the faculty of intellect and intuition.
Chit	consciousness.
Chitta	the faculty of memory and imagination.
Dharma	the principle of order and harmony in the world; the universal law of righteousness; man's spiritual and moral duty.
Gita	song; a shortened form of *Bhagavad Gita.*
Guna	a wave-like principle or mode which pervades the whole of creation. There are three *gunas*, namely *sattva* (harmony), *rajas* (activity) and *tamas* (inertia).
Guru	traditional spiritual teacher.
Jiva	the individual soul.
Karma	action and its consequences, determined by the law of cause and effect.
Manana	reflection on the Truth which has already been heard.
Manas	the lower mind.
Mantram	a traditional prayer or invocation which is repeated with a rosary.

GLOSSARY

Maya
the creative power of the Lord, by means of which the phenomenal world has been brought into existence; cosmic nescience, veiling power which hides the reality of the Self and gives rise to the belief that the manifested world is real.

Nididhyasana
uninterrupted and one-pointed contemplation of the Truth which has been heard and reflected upon.

OM
a sacred syllable, given in the Vedas as the highest name of God; a symbol of the highest reality in its various aspects.

Rajas
the guna of activity and passion-struggle.

Samadhi
unbroken meditation; a high state of consciousness in which the mind transcends the normal subject-object relationship.

Sankalpa
mental activity; the imaginative, picture-making faculty.

Sansara
'ever-flowing', the empirical world in which the jiva lives; the phenomenal universe.

Sanskaras
latent impressions left on the mind by desires, actions and experiences of the past.

GLOSSARY

Sat	existence.
Sat-Chit-Ananda	existence-consciousness-bliss triple designation of *Brahman*.
Sattva	the *guna* of harmony, equilibrium and light.
Shravana	listening to the spiritual Truth.
Tamas	the *guna* of inertia and darkness.
Vasanas	tendencies or urges in the mind, due to latent past impressions and unfulfilled desires (*sanskaras*)
Vedanta	the system of philosophy based on the Upanishads.
Vichara	philosophical enquiry into spiritual Truth.
Viveka	spiritual discrimination between the real and the unreal.
Vritti	a mode of the mind.
Yoga	'union' - the science of the union of man with God; the technique and discipline by means of which the individual soul can achieve conscious union with the supreme spirit.